The Complete 2024
TOWER
Air Fryer
Cookbook for Beginners

1800+ Days of Delicious, Guilt-Free Air Fryer Recipes for Quick & Healthy Meals with UK Ingredients and Measurements

Chelsea Wallace

Copyright© 2024 By Chelsea Wallace

All rights reserved worldwide.

No part of this book may be reproduced or transmitted in any form or by any means, electronic or mechanical, including photo- copying, recording or by any information storage and retrieval system, without written permission from the publisher, except for the inclusion of brief quotations in a review.

Warning-Disclaimer

The purpose of this book is to educate and entertain. The author or publisher does not guarantee that anyone following the techniques, suggestions, tips, ideas, or strategies will become successful. The author and publisher shall have neither liability or responsibility to anyone with respect to any loss or damage caused, or alleged to be caused, directly or indirectly by the information contained in this book.

Table of Contents

INTRODUCTION — 1

Chapter 1   Breakfasts — 3

Chapter 2   Family Favorites — 10

Chapter 3   Fast and Easy Everyday Favourites — 13

Chapter 4   Snacks and Starters — 16

Chapter 5   Beef, Pork, and Lamb — 22

Chapter 6   Poultry — 30

Chapter 7   Fish and Seafood — 39

Chapter 8   Vegetables and Sides — 47

Chapter 9   Vegetarian Mains — 54

Chapter 10   Desserts — 58

Appendix 1   Basic Kitchen Conversions & Equivalents — 62

Appendix 2   Index — 63

INTRODUCTION

Welcome to the world of effortless cooking with the Tower Air Fryer Cookbook! Whether you're a seasoned chef or a busy home cook, this cookbook is your gateway to transforming how you prepare and enjoy meals. The Tower Air Fryer is a game-changer in the kitchen, bringing together the best of modern technology and classic culinary techniques. This introduction will guide you through the essentials of using your air fryer, showcase its versatility, and inspire you with creative recipes that will make cooking easier and more enjoyable.

A Revolution in Cooking

The Tower Air Fryer is more than just a kitchen appliance—it's a revolution in how we approach cooking. By harnessing hot air circulation and a touch of oil, it delivers crispy, golden results without the excessive fat of traditional frying methods. Imagine enjoying your favorite fried foods with up to 80% less fat! The Tower Air Fryer achieves this by using rapid air technology to cook food quickly and evenly, providing that perfect crunch and flavor while retaining essential nutrients.

This innovative appliance offers a healthier alternative without sacrificing taste or texture. Whether you're craving crispy fries, tender chicken wings, or even baked goods, the Tower Air Fryer can handle it all. Its multifunctionality makes it a valuable addition to any kitchen, simplifying meal preparation and offering a range of cooking options from frying and baking to grilling and roasting.

Why Choose the Tower Air Fryer?

One of the key benefits of the Tower Air Fryer is its ability to deliver consistent results with minimal effort. Its user-friendly interface and adjustable temperature settings allow you to customize each dish to your preference. The large capacity means you can cook for a family or batch cook meals for the week ahead. Plus, its sleek design and compact footprint ensure it fits seamlessly into any kitchen space.

The Tower Air Fryer is also designed with convenience in mind. Many models come with removable, non-stick baskets that make cleaning a breeze. And because it uses less oil, you'll spend less time scrubbing away grease and more time enjoying your meals. The appliance's versatility extends beyond traditional frying; you can bake cakes, roast vegetables, and even reheat leftovers with ease. This multifunctional approach means you'll rely less on other kitchen gadgets, streamlining your cooking process and saving valuable counter space.

Getting Started: Tips and Tricks

Before diving into the recipes, it's important to familiarize yourself with your Tower Air Fryer. Start by reading the user manual to understand the specific features and functions of your model. Preheat your air fryer before cooking to ensure even results and use the right amount of oil to achieve that perfect crispy texture. Don't overcrowd the basket; allow space for air circulation to ensure each piece cooks evenly.

Experiment with cooking times and temperatures to find the perfect settings for your favorite dishes. The Tower Air Fryer's quick cooking capabilities might mean you need to adjust your usual recipes. Keep an eye on your food as it cooks and make notes on any adjustments for future reference.

From Breakfast to Dinner: Recipes for Every Meal

This cookbook is designed to make the most out of your Tower Air Fryer, featuring a wide range of recipes from breakfast through dinner and beyond. Each recipe has been carefully crafted to ensure it not only meets the high standards of air frying but also delivers on flavor and nutrition.

Start your day with delicious breakfast options like fluffy air-fried French toast or crispy bacon. For lunch, enjoy healthy yet satisfying meals such as air-fried chicken tenders with a side of roasted vegetables. Dinner doesn't have to be complicated; try easy recipes like air-fried salmon with lemon and herbs or a hearty vegetable stir-fry. Don't forget to explore our snack and dessert sections, where you'll find creative ideas for air-fried treats like crispy churros or apple chips.

Embrace a Healthier Lifestyle

Incorporating the Tower Air Fryer into your cooking routine is not just about enjoying tasty meals; it's also about embracing a healthier lifestyle. By reducing the amount of oil used in cooking, you can lower your calorie intake and make better choices for your overall well-being. This cookbook aims to provide you with delicious recipes that support a balanced diet without compromising on taste.

The Tower Air Fryer allows you to experiment with a variety of ingredients and cooking techniques, making it easier to adopt healthier eating habits. From fresh vegetables and lean proteins to whole grains and wholesome snacks, the recipes in this cookbook will inspire you to cook with confidence and creativity.

Your Culinary Adventure Awaits

We're excited to embark on this culinary adventure with you! The Tower Air Fryer Cookbook is not just a collection of recipes; it's an invitation to explore new flavors, try innovative cooking methods, and enjoy the benefits of a healthier diet. Each recipe has been designed to showcase the versatility of your Tower Air Fryer while delivering mouthwatering results that you and your loved ones will savor.

Get ready to discover the endless possibilities of air frying and elevate your cooking experience. With the Tower Air Fryer Cookbook by your side, you'll be well-equipped to create delicious, nutritious meals with ease. So, roll up your sleeves, fire up your air fryer, and let the cooking begin!

Enjoy the journey and happy cooking!

… Chapter 1

Breakfasts

Western Frittata

Prep time: 10 minutes | Cook time: 19 minutes | Serves 1 to 2

* ½ red or green pepper, cut into ½-inch chunks
* 1 teaspoon rapeseed oil
* 3 eggs, beaten
* 60 g grated Cheddar cheese
* 60 g diced cooked
* gammon
* Salt and freshly ground black pepper, to taste
* 1 teaspoon butter
* 1 teaspoon chopped fresh parsley

1. Preheat the air fryer to 200ºC. 2. Toss the peppers with the rapeseed oil and air fry for 6 minutes, shaking the basket once or twice during the cooking process to redistribute the ingredients. 3. While the vegetables are cooking, beat the eggs well in a bowl, stir in the Cheddar cheese and gammon, and season with salt and freshly ground black pepper. Add the air-fried peppers to this bowl when they have finished cooking. 4. Place a cake pan into the air fryer basket with the butter using an aluminum sling to lower the pan into the basket. Air fry for 1 minute at 190ºC to melt the butter. Remove the cake pan and rotate the pan to distribute the butter and grease the pan. Pour the egg mixture into the cake pan and return the pan to the air fryer, using the aluminum sling. 5. Air fry at 190ºC for 12 minutes, or until the frittata has puffed up and is lightly browned. Let the frittata sit in the air fryer for 5 minutes to cool to an edible temperature and set up. Remove the cake pan from the air fryer, sprinkle with parsley and serve immediately.

Baked Peach Porridge

Prep time: 5 minutes | Cook time: 30 minutes | Serves 6

* rapeseed oil cooking spray
* 475 g certified gluten-free porridge oats
* 475 ml unsweetened almond milk
* 60 ml honey, plus more for drizzling (optional)
* 120 ml non-fat natural
* yoghurt
* 1 teaspoon vanilla extract
* ½ teaspoon ground cinnamon
* ¼ teaspoon salt
* 350 g diced peaches, divided, plus more for serving (optional)

1. Preheat the air fryer to 190ºC. Lightly coat the inside of a 6-inch cake pan with rapeseed oil cooking spray. 2. In a large bowl, mix together the oats, almond milk, honey, yoghurt, vanilla, cinnamon, and salt until well combined. 3. Fold in 180 g peaches and then pour the mixture into the prepared cake pan. 4. Sprinkle the remaining peaches across the top of the porridge mixture. Bake in the air fryer for 30 minutes. 5. Allow to set and cool for 5 minutes before serving with additional fresh fruit and honey for drizzling, if desired.

Cheesy Scrambled Eggs

Prep time: 2 minutes | Cook time: 9 minutes | Serves 2

* 1 teaspoon unsalted butter
* 2 large eggs
* 2 tablespoons milk
* 2 tablespoons grated
* Cheddar cheese
* Salt and freshly ground black pepper, to taste

1. Preheat the air fryer to 150ºC. Place the butter in a baking pan and cook for 1 to 2 minutes, until melted. 2. In a small bowl, whisk together the eggs, milk, and cheese. Season with salt and black pepper. Transfer the mixture to the pan. 3. Cook for 3 minutes. Stir the eggs and push them toward themaize center of the pan. 4. Cook for another 2 minutes, then stir again. Cook for another 2 minutes, until the eggs are just cooked. Serve warm.

Apple Cider Doughnut Holes

Prep time: 10 minutes | Cook time: 6 minutes | Makes 10 mini doughnuts

* Doughnut Holes:
* 175 g plain flour
* 2 tablespoons granulated sugar
* 2 teaspoons baking powder
* 1 teaspoon baking soda
* ½ teaspoon coarse or flaky salt
* Pinch of freshly grated nutmeg
* 60 ml plus 2 tablespoons buttermilk, chilled
* 2 tablespoons apple cider or apple juice, chilled
* 1 large egg, lightly beaten
* Vegetable oil, for brushing
* Glaze:
* 96 g icing sugar
* 2 tablespoons unsweetened apple sauce
* ¼ teaspoon vanilla extract
* Pinch of coarse or flaky salt

1. Make the doughnut holes: In a bowl, whisk together the flour, granulated sugar, baking powder, baking soda, salt, and nutmeg until smooth. Add the buttermilk, cider, and egg and stir with a small rubber spatula or spoon until the dough just comes together. 2. Using a 28 g ice cream scoop or 2 tablespoons, scoop and drop 10 balls of dough into the air fryer basket, spaced evenly apart, and brush the tops lightly with oil. Air fry at 180ºC until the doughnut holes are golden brown and fluffy, about 6 minutes. Transfer the doughnut holes to a wire rack to cool completely. 3. Make the glaze: In a small bowl, stir together the icing sugar, apple sauce, vanilla, and salt until smooth. 4. Dip the tops of the doughnuts holes in the glaze, then let stand until the glaze sets before serving. If you're impatient and want warm doughnuts, have the glaze ready to go while the doughnuts cook, then use the glaze as a dipping sauce for the warm doughnuts, fresh out of the air fryer.

Jalapeño Popper Egg Cups

Prep time: 10 minutes | Cook time: 10 minutes | Serves 2

* 4 large eggs
* 60 g chopped pickled jalapeños
* 60 g full-fat soft cheese
* 120 g grated mature Cheddar cheese

1. In a medium bowl, beat the eggs, then pour into four silicone muffin cups. 2. In a large microwave-safe bowl, place jalapeños, soft cheese, and Cheddar. Microwave for 30 seconds and stir. Take a spoonful, approximately ¼ of the mixture, and place it in the center of one of the egg cups. Repeat with remaining mixture. 3. Place egg cups into the air fryer basket. 4. Adjust the temperature to 160°C and bake for 10 minutes. 5. Serve warm.

Buffalo Chicken Breakfast Muffins

Prep time: 7 minutes | Cook time: 13 to 16 minutes | Serves 10

* 170 g grated cooked chicken
* 85 g blue cheese, crumbled
* 2 tablespoons unsalted butter, melted
* 80 ml Buffalo hot sauce,
* such as Frank's RedHot
* 1 teaspoon minced garlic
* 6 large eggs
* Sea salt and freshly ground black pepper, to taste
* Avocado oil spray

1. In a large bowl, stir together the chicken, blue cheese, melted butter, hot sauce, and garlic. 2. In a medium bowl or large liquid measuring cup, beat the eggs. Season with salt and pepper. 3. Spray 10 silicone muffin cups with oil. Divide the chicken mixture among the cups, and pour the egg mixture over top. 4. Place the cups in the air fryer and set to 150°C. Bake for 13 to 16 minutes, until the muffins are set and cooked through. (Depending on the size of your air fryer, you may need to cook the muffins in batches.)

Banger Egg Cup

Prep time: 10 minutes | Cook time: 15 minutes | Serves 6

* 340 g pork banger, removed from casings
* 6 large eggs
* ½ teaspoon salt
* ¼ teaspoon ground black pepper
* ½ teaspoon crushed red pepper flakes

1. Place banger in six 4-inch ramekins (about 60 g per ramekin) greased with cooking oil. Press banger down to cover bottom and about ½-inch up the sides of ramekins. Crack one egg into each ramekin and sprinkle evenly with salt, black pepper, and red pepper flakes. 2. Place ramekins into air fryer basket. Adjust the temperature to 180°C and set

the timer for 15 minutes. Egg cups will be done when banger is fully cooked to at least 64°C and the egg is firm. Serve warm.

Mozzarella Bacon Calzones

Prep time: 15 minutes | Cook time: 12 minutes | Serves 4

* 2 large eggs
* 120 g blanched finely ground almond flour
* 475 g grated Cheddar cheese
* 60 g soft cheese, softened and broken into small pieces
* 4 slices cooked bacon, crumbled

1. Beat eggs in a small bowl. Pour into a medium nonstick frying pan over medium heat and scramble. Set aside. 2. In a large microwave-safe bowl, mix flour and Mozzarella. Add soft cheese to the bowl. 3. Place bowl in microwave and cook 45 seconds on high to melt cheese, then stir with a fork until a soft dough ball forms. 4. Cut a piece of parchment to fit air fryer basket. Separate dough into two sections and press each out into an 8-inch round. 5. On half of each dough round, place half of the scrambled eggs and crumbled bacon. Fold the other side of the dough over and press to seal the edges. 6. Place calzones on ungreased parchment and into air fryer basket. Adjust the temperature to 180°C and set the timer for 12 minutes, turning calzones halfway through cooking. Crust will be golden and firm when done. 7. Let calzones cool on a cooking rack 5 minutes before serving.

Homemade Toaster Pastries

Prep time: 10 minutes | Cook time: 11 minutes | Makes 6 pastries

* Oil, for spraying
* 1 (425 g) package ready-to-roll pie crust
* 6 tablespoons jam or preserves of choice
* 340 g icing sugar
* 3 tablespoons milk
* 1 to 2 tablespoons sprinkles of choice

1. Preheat the air fryer to 180°C. Line the air fryer basket with parchment and lightly spray with oil. 2. Cut the pie crust into 12 rectangles, about 3 by 4 inches each. You will need to reroll the dough scraps to get 12 rectangles. 3. Spread 1 tablespoon of jam in the centre of 6 rectangles, leaving ¼ inch around the edges. 4. Pour some water into a small bowl. Use your finger to moisten the edge of each rectangle. 5. Top each rectangle with another and use your fingers to press around the edges. Using the prongs of a fork, seal the edges of the dough and poke a few holes in the top of each one. Place the pastries in the prepared basket. 6. Air fry for 11 minutes. Let cool completely. 7. In a medium bowl, whisk together the icing sugar and milk. Spread the icing over the tops of the pastries and add sprinkles. Serve immediately.

Breakfast Banger and Cauliflower

Prep time: 5 minutes | Cook time: 45 minutes | Serves 4

* 450 g banger meat, cooked and crumbled
* 475 ml double/whipping cream
* 1 head cauliflower, chopped
* 235 g grated Cheddar cheese, plus more for topping
* 8 eggs, beaten
* Salt and ground black pepper, to taste

1. Preheat the air fryer to 180ºC. 2. In a large bowl, mix the banger, cream, chopped cauliflower, cheese and eggs. Sprinkle with salt and ground black pepper. 3. Pour the mixture into a greased casserole dish. Bake in the preheated air fryer for 45 minutes or until firm. 4. Top with more Cheddar cheese and serve.

Hearty Honey Yeast Rolls

Prep time: 10 minutes | Cook time: 20 minutes | Makes 8 rolls

* 60 ml whole milk, heated to 46ºC in the microwave
* ½ teaspoon active dry yeast
* 1 tablespoon honey
* 80 g plain flour, plus more for dusting
* ½ teaspoon rock salt
* 2 tablespoons unsalted butter, at room temperature, plus more for greasing
* Flaky sea salt, to taste

1. In a large bowl, whisk together the milk, yeast, and honey and let stand until foamy, about 10 minutes 2.Stir in the flour and salt until just combined 3.Stir in the butter until absorbed 4.Scrape the dough onto a lightly floured work surface and knead until smooth, about 6 minutes 5.Transfer the dough to a lightly greased bowl, cover loosely with a sheet of plastic wrap or a kitchen towel, and let sit until nearly doubled in size, about 1 hour 6.Uncover the dough, lightly press it down to expel the bubbles, then portion it into 8 equal pieces 7.Prep the work surface by wiping it clean with a damp paper towel (if there is flour on the work surface, it will prevent the dough from sticking lightly to the surface, which helps it form a ball) 8.Roll each piece into a ball by cupping the palm of the hand around the dough against the work surface and moving the heel of the hand in a circular motion while using the thumb to contain the dough and tighten it into a perfectly round ball 9.Once all the balls are formed, nestle them side by side in the air fryer basket 10.Cover the rolls loosely with a kitchen towel or a sheet of plastic wrap and let sit until lightly risen and puffed, 20 to 30 minutes 11.Preheat the air fryer to 130ºC 12.Uncover the rolls and gently brush with more butter, being careful not to press the rolls too hard 13.Air fry until the rolls are light golden brown and fluffy, about 12 minutes 14.Remove the rolls from the air fryer and brush liberally with more butter, if you like, and sprinkle each roll with a pinch of sea salt 15.Serve warm.

Mushroom-and-Tomato Stuffed Hash Browns

Prep time: 10 minutes | Cook time: 20 minutes | Serves 4

* rapeseed oil cooking spray
* 1 tablespoon plus 2 teaspoons rapeseed oil, divided
* 110 g baby mushrooms, diced
* 1 spring onion, white parts and green parts, diced
* 1 garlic clove, minced
* 475 g grated potatoes
* ½ teaspoon salt
* ¼ teaspoon black pepper
* 1 plum tomato, diced
* 120 g grated mozzarella

1. Preheat the air fryer to 190ºC. Lightly coat the inside of a 6-inch cake pan with rapeseed oil cooking spray. 2. In a small frying pan, heat 2 teaspoons rapeseed oil over medium heat. Add the mushrooms, spring onion, and garlic, and cook for 4 to 5 minutes, or until they have softened and are beginning to show some color. Remove from heat. 3. Meanwhile, in a large bowl, combine the potatoes, salt, pepper, and the remaining tablespoon rapeseed oil. Toss until all potatoes are well coated. 4. Pour half of the potatoes into the bottom of the cake pan. Top with the mushroom mixture, tomato, and mozzarella. Spread the remaining potatoes over the top. 5. Bake in the air fryer for 12 to 15 minutes, or until the top is golden brown. 6. Remove from the air fryer and allow to cool for 5 minutes before slicing and serving.

Drop Biscuits

Prep time: 10 minutes | Cook time: 9 to 10 minutes | Serves 5

* 500 g plain flour
* 1 tablespoon baking powder
* 1 tablespoon sugar (optional)
* 1 teaspoon salt
* 6 tablespoons butter, plus more for brushing on the biscuits (optional)
* 180 ml buttermilk
* 1 to 2 tablespoons oil

1. In a large bowl, whisk the flour, baking powder, sugar (if using), and salt until blended. 2. Add the butter. Using a pastry cutter or 2 forks, work the dough until pea-size balls of the butter-flour mixture appear. Stir in the buttermilk until the mixture is sticky. 3. Preheat the air fryer to 170ºC. Line the air fryer basket with parchment paper and spritz it with oil. 4. Drop the dough by the tablespoonful onto the prepared basket, leaving 1 inch between each, to form 10 biscuits. 5. Bake for 5 minutes. Flip the biscuits and cook for 4 minutes more for a light brown top, or 5 minutes more for a darker biscuit. Brush the tops with melted butter, if desired.

Pancake Cake

Prep time: 10 minutes | Cook time: 7 minutes | Serves 4

* 60 g blanched finely ground almond flour
* 30 g powdered erythritol
* ½ teaspoon baking powder
* 2 tablespoons unsalted butter, softened
* 1 large egg
* ½ teaspoon unflavoured gelatin
* ½ teaspoon vanilla extract
* ½ teaspoon ground cinnamon

1. In a large bowl, mix almond flour, erythritol, and baking powder. Add butter, egg, gelatin, vanilla, and cinnamon. Pour into a round baking pan. 2. Place pan into the air fryer basket. 3. Adjust the temperature to 150ºC and set the timer for 7 minutes. 4. When the cake is completely cooked, a toothpick will come out clean. Cut cake into four and serve.

Everything Bagels

Prep time: 15 minutes | Cook time: 14 minutes | Makes 6 bagels

* 415 g grated Cheddar cheese or goat cheese Mozzarella
* 2 tablespoons unsalted butter or coconut oil
* 1 large egg, beaten
* 1 tablespoon apple cider vinegar
* 120 g blanched almond flour
* 1 tablespoon baking powder
* ⅛ teaspoon fine sea salt
* 1½ teaspoons sesame seeds or za'atar

1. Make the dough: Put the Mozzarella and butter in a large microwave-safe bowl and microwave for 1 to 2 minutes, until the cheese is entirely melted. Stir well. Add the egg and vinegar. Using a hand mixer on medium, combine well. Add the almond flour, baking powder, and salt and, using the mixer, combine well. 2. Lay a piece of parchment paper on the countertop and place the dough on it. Knead it for about 3 minutes. The dough should be a little sticky but pliable. (If the dough is too sticky, chill it in the refrigerator for an hour or overnight.) 3. Preheat the air fryer to 180ºC. Spray a baking sheet or pie dish that will fit into your air fryer with avocado oil. 4. Divide the dough into 6 equal portions. Roll 1 portion into a log that is 6 inches long and about ½ inch thick. Form the log into a circle and seal the edges together, making a bagel shape. Repeat with the remaining portions of dough, making 6 bagels. 5. Place the bagels on the greased baking sheet. Spray the bagels with avocado oil and top with everything bagel seasoning, pressing the seasoning into the dough with your hands. 6. Place the bagels in the air fryer and bake for 14 minutes, or until cooked through and golden brown, flipping after 6 minutes. 7. Remove the bagels from the air fryer and allow them to cool slightly before slicing

them in half and serving. Store leftovers in an airtight container in the fridge for up to 4 days or in the freezer for up to a month.

Honey-Apricot Muesli with Greek Yoghurt

Prep time: 10 minutes | Cook time: 30 minutes | Serves 6

* 235 g porridge oats
* 60 g dried apricots, diced
* 60 g almond slivers
* 60 g walnuts, chopped
* 60 g pumpkin seeds
* 60 to 80 ml honey, plus more for drizzling
* 1 tablespoon rapeseed oil
* 1 teaspoon ground
* cinnamon
* ¼ teaspoon ground nutmeg
* ¼ teaspoon salt
* 2 tablespoons sugar-free dark chocolate crisps (optional)
* 700 ml fat-free natural yoghurt

1. Preheat the air fryer to 130ºC. Line the air fryer basket with parchment paper. 2. In a large bowl, combine the oats, apricots, almonds, walnuts, pumpkin seeds, honey, rapeseed oil, cinnamon, nutmeg, and salt, mixing so that the honey, oil, and spices are well distributed. 3. Pour the mixture onto the parchment paper and spread it into an even layer. 4. Bake for 10 minutes, then shake or stir and spread back out into an even layer. Continue baking for 10 minutes more, then repeat the process of shaking or stirring the mixture. Bake for an additional 10 minutes before removing from the air fryer. 5. Allow the muesli to cool completely before stirring in the chocolate crisps (if using) and pouring into an airtight container for storage. 6. For each serving, top 120 ml Greek yoghurt with 80 ml muesli and a drizzle of honey, if needed.

Asparagus and Pepper Strata

Prep time: 10 minutes | Cook time: 14 to 20 minutes | Serves 4

* 8 large asparagus spears, trimmed and cut into 2-inch pieces
* 80 g grated carrot
* 120 g chopped red pepper
* 2 slices wholemeal bread,
* cut into ½-inch cubes
* 3 egg whites
* 1 egg
* 3 tablespoons 1% milk
* ½ teaspoon dried thyme

1. In a baking pan, combine the asparagus, carrot, red pepper, and 1 tablespoon of water. Bake in the air fryer at 170ºC for 3 to 5 minutes, or until crisp-tender. Drain well. 2. Add the bread cubes to the vegetables and gently toss. 3. In a medium bowl, whisk the egg whites, egg, milk, and thyme until frothy. 4. Pour the egg mixture into the pan. Bake for 11 to 15 minutes, or until the strata is slightly puffy and set and the top starts to brown. Serve.

Parmesan Banger Egg Muffins

Prep time: 5 minutes | Cook time: 20 minutes | Serves 4

* 170 g Italian-seasoned banger, sliced
* 6 eggs
* 30 ml double cream
* Salt and ground black pepper, to taste
* 85 g Parmesan cheese, grated

1. Preheat the air fryer to 180ºC. Grease a muffin pan. 2. Put the sliced banger in the muffin pan. 3. Beat the eggs with the cream in a bowl and season with salt and pepper. 4. Pour half of the mixture over the bangers in the pan. 5. Sprinkle with cheese and the remaining egg mixture. 6. Bake in the preheated air fryer for 20 minutes or until set. 7. Serve immediately.

Pitta and Pepperoni Pizza

Prep time: 10 minutes | Cook time: 6 minutes | Serves 1

* 1 teaspoon rapeseed oil
* 1 tablespoon pizza sauce
* 1 pitta bread
* 6 pepperoni slices
* 60 g grated Cheddar cheese
* ¼ teaspoon garlic powder
* ¼ teaspoon dried oregano

1. Preheat the air fryer to 180ºC. Grease the air fryer basket with rapeseed oil. 2. Spread the pizza sauce on top of the pitta bread. Put the pepperoni slices over the sauce, followed by the Cheddar cheese. 3. Season with garlic powder and oregano. 4. Put the pitta pizza inside the air fryer and place a trivet on top. 5. Bake in the preheated air fryer for 6 minutes and serve.

Banger and Egg Breakfast Burrito

Prep time: 5 minutes | Cook time: 30 minutes | Serves 6

* 6 eggs
* Salt and pepper, to taste
* Cooking oil
* 120 g chopped red pepper
* 120 g chopped green pepper
* 230 g chicken banger
* meat (removed from casings)
* 120 ml tomato salsa
* 6 medium (8-inch) wheat maize wraps
* 120 g grated Cheddar cheese

1. In a medium bowl, whisk the eggs. Add salt and pepper to taste. 2. Place a frying pan on medium-high heat. Spray with cooking oil. Add the eggs. Scramble for 2 to 3 minutes, until the eggs are fluffy. Remove the eggs from the frying pan and set aside. 3. If needed, spray the frying pan with more oil. Add the chopped red and green peppers. Cook for 2 to 3 minutes, until the peppers are soft. 4. Add the banger meat to the frying pan. Break the banger into smaller pieces using a spatula or spoon. Cook for 3 to 4 minutes, until the banger is brown. 5. Add the tomato salsa and scrambled eggs. Stir to combine. Remove the frying pan from heat. 6. Spoon the mixture evenly onto the maize wraps. 7. To form the burritos, fold the sides of each maize wrap in toward the middle and then roll up from the bottom. You tin secure each burrito with a toothpick. Or you tin moisten the outside edge of the maize wrap with a small amount of water. I prefer to use a cooking brush, but you tin also dab with your fingers. 8. Spray the burritos with cooking oil and place them in the air fryer. Do not stack. Cook the burritos in batches if they do not all fit in the basket. Air fry at 200ºC for 8 minutes. 9. Open the air fryer and flip the burritos. Cook for an additional 2 minutes or until crisp. 10. If necessary, repeat steps 8 and 9 for the remaining burritos. 11. Sprinkle the Cheddar cheese over the burritos. Cool before serving.

Classic British Breakfast

Prep time: 5 minutes | Cook time: 25 minutes | Serves 2

* 235 g potatoes, sliced and diced
* 475 g baked beans
* 2 eggs
* 1 tablespoon rapeseed oil
* 1 banger
* Salt, to taste

1. Preheat the air fryer to 200ºC and allow to warm. 2. Break the eggs onto a baking dish and sprinkle with salt. 3. Lay the beans on the dish, next to the eggs. 4. In a bowl, coat the potatoes with the rapeseed oil. Sprinkle with salt. 5. Transfer the bowl of potato slices to the air fryer and bake for 10 minutes. 6. Swap out the bowl of potatoes for the dish containing the eggs and beans. Bake for another 10 minutes. Cover the potatoes with parchment paper. 7. Slice up the banger and throw the slices on top of the beans and eggs. Bake for another 5 minutes. 8. Serve with the potatoes.

Spinach Omelet

Prep time: 5 minutes | Cook time: 12 minutes | Serves 2

* 4 large eggs
* 350 g chopped fresh spinach leaves
* 2 tablespoons peeled and chopped brown onion
* 2 tablespoons salted butter, melted
* 120 g grated mild Cheddar cheese
* ¼ teaspoon salt

1. In an ungreased round nonstick baking dish, whisk eggs. Stir in spinach, onion, butter, Cheddar, and salt. 2. Place dish into air fryer basket. Adjust the temperature to 160ºC and bake for 12 minutes. Omelet will be done when browned on the top and firm in the middle. 3. Slice in half and serve warm on two medium plates.

Tomato and Cheddar Rolls

Prep time: 30 minutes | Cook time: 25 minutes | Makes 12 rolls

* 4 vine tomatoes
* ½ clove garlic, minced
* 1 tablespoon rapeseed oil
* ¼ teaspoon dried thyme
* Salt and freshly ground black pepper, to taste
* 500 g plain flour
* 1 teaspoon fast-action
* yeast
* 2 teaspoons sugar
* 2 teaspoons salt
* 1 tablespoon rapeseed oil
* 235 g grated Cheddar cheese, plus more for sprinkling at the end
* 350 ml water

1. Cut the tomatoes in half, remove the seeds with your fingers and transfer to a bowl. Add the garlic, rapeseed oil, dried thyme, salt and freshly ground black pepper and toss well. 2. Preheat the air fryer to 200°C. 3. Place the tomatoes, cut side up in the air fryer basket and air fry for 10 minutes. The tomatoes should just start to brown. Shake the basket to redistribute the tomatoes, and air fry for another 5 to 10 minutes at 170°C until the tomatoes are no longer juicy. Let the tomatoes cool and then rough chop them. 4. Combine the flour, yeast, sugar and salt in the bowl of a stand mixer. Add the rapeseed oil, chopped roasted tomatoes and Cheddar cheese to the flour mixture and start to mix using the dough hook attachment. As you're mixing, add 300 ml of the water, mixing until the dough comes together. Continue to knead the dough with the dough hook for another 10 minutes, adding enough water to the dough to get it to the right consistency. 5. Transfer the dough to an oiled bowl, cover with a clean kitchen towel and let it rest and rise until it has doubled in volume, about 1 to 2 hours. Then, divide the dough into 12 equal portions. Roll each portion of dough into a ball. Lightly coat each dough ball with oil and let the dough balls rest and rise a second time, covered lightly with cling film for 45 minutes. (Alternately, you tin place the rolls in the refrigerator overnight and take them out 2 hours before you bake them.) 6. Preheat the air fryer to 180°C. 7. Spray the dough balls and the air fryer basket with a little rapeseed oil. Place three rolls at a time in the basket and bake for 10 minutes. Add a little grated Cheddar cheese on top of the rolls for the last 2 minutes of air frying for an attractive finish.

Breakfast Meatballs

Prep time: 10 minutes | Cook time: 15 minutes | Makes 18 meatballs

* 450 g pork banger meat, removed from casings
* ½ teaspoon salt
* ¼ teaspoon ground black pepper
* 120 g grated mature Cheddar cheese
* 30 g soft cheese, softened
* 1 large egg, whisked

1. Combine all ingredients in a large bowl. Form mixture into eighteen 1-inch meatballs. 2. Place meatballs into ungreased air fryer basket. Adjust the temperature to 200°C and air fry for 15 minutes, shaking basket three times during cooking. Meatballs will be browned on the outside and have an internal temperature of at least 64°C when completely cooked. Serve warm.

Eggnog Bread

Prep time: 10 minutes | Cook time: 18 minutes | Serves 6 to 8

* 120 g flour, plus more for dusting
* 35 g sugar
* 1 teaspoon baking powder
* ¼ teaspoon salt
* ¼ teaspoon nutmeg
* 120 ml eggnog
* 1 egg yolk
* 1 tablespoon plus 1 teaspoon butter, melted
* 60 g pecans
* 60 g chopped candied fruit (cherries, pineapple, or mixed fruits)
* Cooking spray

1. Preheat the air fryer to 180°C 2.In a medium bowl, stir together the flour, sugar, baking powder, salt, and nutmeg 3.Add eggnog, egg yolk, and butter 4.Mix well but do not beat 5.Stir in nuts and fruit 6.Spray a baking dish with cooking spray and dust with flour 7.Spread batter into prepared pan and bake for 18 minutes or until top is dark golden brown and bread starts to pull away from sides of pan 8.Serve immediately.

Gluten-Free Muesli Cereal

Prep time: 7 minutes | Cook time: 30 minutes | Makes 820 ml

* Oil, for spraying
* 350 g gluten-free porridge oats
* 120 g chopped walnuts
* 120 g chopped almonds
* 120 g pumpkin seeds
* 60 ml maple syrup or honey
* 1 tablespoon toasted sesame oil or vegetable oil
* 1 teaspoon ground cinnamon
* ½ teaspoon salt
* 120 g dried cranberries

1. Preheat the air fryer to 120°C. Line the air fryer basket with parchment and spray lightly with oil. (Do not skip the step of lining the basket; the parchment will keep the muesli from falling through the holes.) 2. In a large bowl, mix together the oats, walnuts, almonds, pumpkin seeds, maple syrup, sesame oil, cinnamon, and salt. 3. Spread the mixture in an even layer in the prepared basket. 4. Cook for 30 minutes, stirring every 10 minutes. 5. Transfer the muesli to a bowl, add the dried cranberries, and toss to combine. 6. Let cool to room temperature before storing in an airtight container.

Chapter 2
Family Favorites

Mixed Berry Crumble

Prep time: 10 minutes | Cook time: 11 to 16 minutes | Serves 4

* 120 g chopped fresh strawberries
* 120 g fresh blueberries
* 80 g frozen raspberries
* 1 tablespoon freshly squeezed lemon juice
* 1 tablespoon honey
* 80 g wholemeal plain flour
* 3 tablespoons light muscovado sugar
* 2 tablespoons unsalted butter, melted

1. In a baking pan, combine the strawberries, blueberries, and raspberries. 2.Drizzle with the lemon juice and honey. 3.In a small bowl, mix the pastry flour and brown sugar. 4.Stir in the butter and mix until crumbly. 5.Sprinkle this mixture over the fruit. 6.Bake at 190°C for 11 to 16 minutes, or until the fruit is tender and bubbly and the topping is golden brown. 7.Serve warm.

Berry Cheesecake

Prep time: 5 minutes | Cook time: 10 minutes | Serves 4

* Oil, for spraying
* 227 g soft white cheese
* 6 tablespoons sugar
* 1 tablespoon sour cream
* 1 large egg
* ½ teaspoon vanilla extract
* ¼ teaspoon lemon juice
* 120 g fresh mixed berries

1. Preheat the air fryer to 180°C. 2.Line the air fryer basket with parchment and spray lightly with oil. 3.In a blender, combine the soft white cheese, sugar, sour cream, egg, vanilla, and lemon juice and blend until smooth. 4.Pour the mixture into a 4-inch springform pan. 5.Place the pan in the prepared basket. Cook for 8 to 10 minutes, or until only the very centre jiggles slightly when the pan is moved. 6.Refrigerate the cheesecake in the pan for at least 2 hours. 7.Release the sides from the springform pan, top the cheesecake with the mixed berries, and serve.

Steak and Vegetable Kebabs

Prep time: 15 minutes | Cook time: 5 to 7 minutes | Serves 4

* 2 tablespoons balsamic vinegar
* 2 teaspoons olive oil
* ½ teaspoon dried marjoram
* ⅛ teaspoon ground black
* pepper
* 340 g silverside, cut into 1-inch pieces
* 1 red pepper, sliced
* 16 button mushrooms
* 235 g cherry tomatoes

1. In a medium bowl, stir together the balsamic vinegar, olive oil, marjoram, and black pepper. 2.Add the steak and stir to coat. Let stand for 10 minutes at room temperature. 3.Alternating items, thread the beef, red pepper, mushrooms, and tomatoes onto 8 bamboo or metal skewers that fit in the air fryer. 4.Air fry at 200°C for 5 to 7 minutes, or until the beef is browned and reaches at least 64°C on a meat thermometer. 5.Serve immediately.

Puffed Egg Tarts

Prep time: 10 minutes | Cook time: 42 minutes | Makes 4 tarts

* Oil, for spraying
* Plain flour, for dusting
* 1 (340 g) sheet frozen puff pastry, thawed
* 180 g shredded Cheddar cheese, divided
* 4 large eggs
* 2 teaspoons chopped fresh parsley
* Salt and ground black pepper, to taste

1. Preheat the air fryer to 200°C. 2.Line the air fryer basket with parchment and spray lightly with oil. Lightly dust your work surface with flour. 3.Unfold the puff pastry and cut it into 4 equal squares. 4.Place 2 squares in the prepared basket. Cook for 10 minutes. 5.Remove the basket. Press the centre of each tart shell with a spoon to make an indentation. 6.Sprinkle 3 tablespoons of cheese into each indentation and crack 1 egg into the centre of each tart shell. 7.Cook for another 7 to 11 minutes, or until the eggs are cooked to your desired doneness. 8.Repeat with the remaining puff pastry squares, cheese, and eggs. 9.Sprinkle evenly with the parsley, and season with salt and black pepper. 10.Serve immediately.

Pork Burgers with Red Cabbage Salad

Prep time: 20 minutes | Cook time: 7 to 9 minutes | Serves 4

* 120 ml Greek yoghurt
* 2 tablespoons low-salt mustard, divided
* 1 tablespoon lemon juice
* 60 g sliced red cabbage
* 60 g grated carrots
* 450 g lean finely chopped
* pork
* ½ teaspoon paprika
* 235 g mixed salad leaves
* 2 small tomatoes, sliced
* 8 small low-salt wholemeal sandwich buns, cut in half

1. In a small bowl, combine the yoghurt, 1 tablespoon mustard, lemon juice, cabbage, and carrots; mix and refrigerate. 2.In a medium bowl, combine the pork, remaining 1 tablespoon mustard, and paprika. Form into 8 small patties. Put the sliders into the air fryer basket. 3.Air fry at 200°C for 7 to 9 minutes, or until the sliders register 74°C as tested with a meat thermometer. 4.Assemble the burgers by placing some of the lettuce greens on a bun bottom. 5.Top with a tomato slice, the burgers, and the cabbage mixture. 6.Add the bun top and serve immediately.

Chapter 2 Family Favorites 11

Cheesy Roasted Sweet Potatoes

Prep time: 7 minutes | Cook time: 18 to 23 minutes | Serves 4

* 2 large sweet potatoes, peeled and sliced
* 1 teaspoon olive oil
* 1 tablespoon white
* balsamic vinegar
* 1 teaspoon dried thyme
* 60 g Parmesan cheese

1. In a large bowl, drizzle the sweet potato slices with the olive oil and toss. 2.Sprinkle with the balsamic vinegar and thyme and toss again. 3.Sprinkle the potatoes with the Parmesan cheese and toss to coat. 4.Roast the slices, in batches, in the air fryer basket at 200ºC for 18 to 23 minutes, tossing the sweet potato slices in the basket once during cooking, until tender. 5.Repeat with the remaining sweet potato slices. 6.Serve immediately.

Veggie Tuna Melts

Prep time: 15 minutes | Cook time: 7 to 11 minutes | Serves 4

* 2 low-salt wholemeal English muffins, split
* 1 (170 g) tin chunk light low-salt tuna, drained
* 235 g shredded carrot
* 80 g chopped mushrooms
* 2 spring onions, white
* and green parts, sliced
* 80 ml fat-free Greek yoghurt
* 2 tablespoons low-salt wholegrain mustard
* 2 slices low-salt low-fat Swiss cheese, halved

1. Place the English muffin halves in the air fryer basket. 2.Air fry at 170ºC for 3 to 4 minutes, or until crisp. Remove from the basket and set aside. 3.In a medium bowl, thoroughly mix the tuna, carrot, mushrooms, spring onions, yoghurt, and mustard. 4.Top each half of the muffins with one-fourth of the tuna mixture and a half slice of Swiss cheese. 5.Air fry for 4 to 7 minutes, or until the tuna mixture is hot and the cheese melts and starts to brown. 6.Serve immediately.

Coconut Chicken Tenders

Prep time: 10 minutes | Cook time: 12 minutes | Serves 4

* Oil, for spraying
* 2 large eggs
* 60 ml milk
* 1 tablespoon chilli sauce
* 350 g sweetened desiccated coconut
* 90 g Japanese breadcrumbs
* 1 teaspoon salt
* ½ teaspoon ground black pepper
* 450 g chicken tenders

1. Line the air fryer basket with parchment and spray lightly with oil. 2.In a small bowl, whisk together the eggs, milk, and chili sauce. 3.In a shallow dish, mix together the coconut, breadcrumbs, salt, and black pepper. 4.Coat the chicken in the egg mix, then dredge in the coconut mixture until evenly coated. 5.Place the chicken in the prepared basket and spray liberally with oil. 6.Air fry at 200ºC for 6 minutes, flip, spray with more oil, and cook for another 6 minutes, or until the internal temperature reaches 74ºC.

Pecan Rolls

Prep time: 20 minutes | Cook time: 20 to 24 minutes | Makes 12 rolls

* 220 g plain flour, plus more for dusting
* 2 tablespoons caster sugar, plus 60 ml, divided
* 1 teaspoon salt
* 3 tablespoons butter, at room temperature
* 180 ml milk, whole or
* semi-skimmed
* 40 g packed light muscovado sugar
* 120g chopped pecans, toasted
* 1 to 2 tablespoons oil
* 35g icing sugar (optional)

1. In a large bowl, whisk the flour, 2 tablespoons caster sugar, and salt until blended. 2.Stir in the butter and milk briefly until a sticky dough form. In a small bowl, stir together the brown sugar and remaining 60 g caster sugar. 3.Place a piece of parchment paper on a work surface and dust it with flour. Roll the dough on the prepared surface to ¼ inch thickness. 4.Spread the sugar mixture over the dough. Sprinkle the pecans on top. Roll up the dough jam roll-style, pinching the ends to seal. 5.Cut the dough into 12 rolls. Preheat the air fryer to 160ºC. 6.Line the air fryer basket with parchment paper and spritz the parchment with oil. Place 6 rolls on the prepared parchment. Bake for 5 minutes. 7.Flip the rolls and bake for 5 to 7 minutes more until lightly browned. Repeat with the remaining rolls. 8.Sprinkle with icing sugar (if using).

Meringue Cookies

Prep time: 15 minutes | Cook time: 1 hour 30 minutes | Makes 20 cookies

* Oil, for spraying
* 4 large egg whites
* 185 g sugar
* Pinch cream of tartar

1. Preheat the air fryer to 60ºC. 2.Line the air fryer basket with parchment and spray lightly with oil. 3.In a small heatproof bowl, whisk together the egg whites and sugar. 4.Fill a small saucepan halfway with water, place it over medium heat, and bring to a light simmer. 5.Place the bowl with the egg whites on the saucepan, making sure the bottom of the bowl does not touch the water. 6.Whisk the mixture until the sugar is dissolved. Transfer the mixture to a large bowl and add the cream of tartar. 7.Using an electric mixer, beat the mixture on high until it is glossy and stiff peaks form. 8.Transfer the mixture to a piping bag or a zip-top plastic bag with a corner cut off. Pipe rounds into the prepared basket. 9.You may need to work in batches, depending on the size of your air fryer. Cook for 1 hour 30 minutes. 10.Turn off the air fryer and let the meringues cool completely inside. 11.The residual heat will continue to dry them out.

Chapter 3
Fast and Easy Everyday Favourites

Red Lentil and Goat Cheese Stuffed Tomatoes

Prep time: 10 minutes | Cook time: 15 minutes | Serves 4

* 4 tomatoes
* 120 ml cooked red lentils
* 1 garlic clove, minced
* 1 tablespoon minced red onion
* 4 basil leaves, minced
* ¼ teaspoon salt
* ¼ teaspoon black pepper
* 110 g goat cheese
* 2 tablespoons shredded Parmesan cheese

1. Preheat the air fryer to 192°C. 2. Slice the top off of each tomato. Using a knife and spoon, cut and scoop out half of the flesh inside of the tomato. 3. Place it into a medium bowl. To the bowl with the tomato, add the cooked lentils, garlic, onion, basil, salt, pepper, and goat cheese. Stir until well combined. 4. Spoon the filling into the scooped-out cavity of each of the tomatoes, then top each one with ½ tablespoon of shredded Parmesan cheese. 5. Place the tomatoes in a single layer in the air fryer basket and bake for 15 minutes.

Simple Pea Delight

Prep time: 5 minutes | Cook time: 15 minutes | Serves 2 to 4

* 120 g flour
* 1 teaspoon baking powder
* 3 eggs
* 235 ml coconut milk
* 235 g soft white cheese
* 3 tablespoons pea protein
* 120 g chicken or turkey strips
* Pinch of sea salt
* 235 g Mozzarella cheese

1. Preheat the air fryer to 200°C. 2.In a large bowl, mix all ingredients together using a large wooden spoon. 3.Spoon equal amounts of the mixture into muffin cups and bake for 15 minutes. 4.Serve immediately.

Beery and Crunchy Onion Rings

Prep time: 10 minutes | Cook time: 16 minutes | Serves 2 to 4

* 80 g plain flour
* 1 teaspoon paprika
* ½ teaspoon bicarbonate of soda
* 1 teaspoon salt
* ½ teaspoon freshly ground black pepper
* 1 egg, beaten
* 180 ml beer
* 175 g breadcrumbs
* 1 tablespoons olive oil
* 1 large Vidalia or sweet onion, peeled and sliced into ½-inch rings
* Cooking spray

1. Preheat the air fryer to 180°C. Spritz the air fryer basket with cooking spray. 2. Combine the flour, paprika, bicarbonate of soda, salt, and ground black pepper in a bowl. Stir to mix well. 3. Combine the egg and beer in a separate bowl. Stir to mix well. 4 Make a well in the centre of the flour mixture, then pour the egg mixture in the well. Stir to mix everything well. 5. Pour the breadcrumbs and olive oil in a shallow plate. Stir to mix well. 6. Dredge the onion rings gently into the flour and egg mixture, then shake the excess off and put into the plate of breadcrumbs. 7. Flip to coat both sides well. 8 Arrange the onion rings in the preheated air fryer. Air fry in batches for 16 minutes or until golden brown and crunchy. 9. Flip the rings and put the bottom rings to the top halfway through. Serve immediately.

Southwest Corn and Pepper Roast

Prep time: 10 minutes | Cook time: 10 minutes | Serves 4

* For the Corn:
* 350 g thawed frozen corn kernels
* 235 g mixed diced peppers
* 1 jalapeño, diced
* 235 g diced brown onion
* ½ teaspoon ancho chilli powder
* 1 tablespoon fresh lemon
* juice
* 1 teaspoon ground cumin
* ½ teaspoon rock salt
* Cooking spray
* For Serving:
* 60 g feta cheese
* 60 g chopped fresh coriander
* 1 tablespoon fresh lemon juice

1. Preheat the air fryer to 190°C 2.Spritz the air fryer with cooking spray 3.Combine the ingredients for the corn in a large bowl 4.Stir to mix well 5.Pour the mixture into the air fryer 6.Air fry for 10 minutes or until the corn and peppers are soft 7.Shake the basket halfway through the cooking time 8.Transfer them onto a large plate, then spread with feta cheese and coriander 9.Drizzle with lemon juice and serve.

Peppery Brown Rice Fritters

Prep time: 10 minutes | Cook time: 8 to 10 minutes | Serves 4

* 1 (284 g) bag frozen cooked brown rice, thawed
* 1 egg
* 3 tablespoons brown rice flour
* 80 g finely grated carrots
* 80 g minced red pepper
* 2 tablespoons minced fresh basil
* 3 tablespoons grated Parmesan cheese
* 2 teaspoons olive oil

1. Preheat the air fryer to 190°C. 2.In a small bowl, combine the thawed rice, egg, and flour and mix to blend. 3.Stir in the carrots, pepper, basil, and Parmesan cheese. 4.Form the mixture into 8 fritters and drizzle with the olive oil. 5.Put the fritters carefully into the air fryer basket. 6.Air fry for 8 to 10 minutes, or until the fritters are golden brown and cooked through. 7.Serve immediately.

Scalloped Veggie Mix

Prep time: 10 minutes | Cook time: 15 minutes | Serves 4

* 1 Yukon Gold or other small white potato, thinly sliced
* 1 small sweet potato, peeled and thinly sliced
* 1 medium carrot, thinly sliced
* 60 g minced onion
* 3 garlic cloves, minced
* 180 ml 2 percent milk
* 2 tablespoons cornflour
* ½ teaspoon dried thyme

1. Preheat the air fryer to 190ºC. 2.In a baking tray, layer the potato, sweet potato, carrot, onion, and garlic. 3.In a small bowl, whisk the milk, cornflour, and thyme until blended. 4.Pour the milk mixture evenly over the vegetables in the pan. Bake for 15 minutes. 5.Check the casserole—it should be golden brown on top, and the vegetables should be tender. 6.Serve immediately.

Easy Devils on Horseback

Prep time: 5 minutes | Cook time: 7 minutes | Serves 12

* 24 small pitted prunes (128 g)
* 60 g crumbled blue cheese, divided
* 8 slices middle bacon, cut crosswise into thirds

1. Preheat the air fryer to 200ºC. 2.Halve the prunes lengthwise, but don't cut them all the way through. 3.Place ½ teaspoon of cheese in the centre of each prune. 4.Wrap a piece of bacon around each prune and secure the bacon with a toothpick. 5.Working in batches, arrange a single layer of the prunes in the air fryer basket. 6.Air fry for about 7 minutes, flipping halfway, until the bacon is cooked through and crisp. 7.Let cool slightly and serve warm.

Simple and Easy Croutons

Prep time: 5 minutes | Cook time: 8 minutes | Serves 4

* 2 sliced bread
* 1 tablespoon olive oil
* Hot soup, for serving

1. Preheat the air fryer to 200ºC. 2.Cut the slices of bread into medium-size chunks. 3.Brush the air fryer basket with the oil. 4.Place the chunks inside and air fry for at least 8 minutes. 5.Serve with hot soup.

Cheesy Jalapeño Cornbread

Prep time: 10 minutes | Cook time: 20 minutes | Serves 8

* 160 ml cornmeal
* 80 ml plain flour
* ¾ teaspoon baking powder
* 2 tablespoons margarine, melted
* ½ teaspoon rock salt
* 1 tablespoon granulated sugar
* 180 ml whole milk
* 1 large egg, beaten
* 1 red chilli, thinly sliced
* 80 ml shredded extra mature Cheddar cheese
* Cooking spray

1. Preheat the air fryer to 152ºC. Spritz the air fryer basket with cooking spray. 2.Combine all the ingredients in a large bowl. Stir to mix well. Pour the mixture in a baking pan. 3.Arrange the pan in the preheated air fryer. Bake for 20 minutes or until a toothpick inserted in the centre of the bread comes out clean. 4.When the cooking is complete, remove the baking pan from the air fryer and allow the bread to cool for a few minutes before slicing to serve.

Baked Chorizo Scotch Eggs

* Prep time:5 minutes | Cook time: 15 to 20 minutes | Makes 4 eggs
* 450 g Mexican chorizo or other seasoned banger meat
* 4 soft-boiled eggs plus 1 raw egg
* 1 tablespoon water
* 120 ml plain flour
* 235 ml panko breadcrumbs
* Cooking spray

1. Divide the chorizo into 4 equal portions. Flatten each portion into a disc. Place a soft-boiled egg in the centre of each disc. Wrap the chorizo around the egg, encasing it completely. Place the encased eggs on a plate and chill for at least 30 minutes. 2.Preheat the air fryer to 182ºC. 3.Beat the raw egg with 1 tablespoon of water. Place the flour on a small plate and the panko on a second plate. Working with 1 egg at a time, roll the encased egg in the flour, then dip it in the egg mixture. Dredge the egg in the panko and place on a plate. Repeat with the remaining eggs. 4.Spray the eggs with oil and place in the air fryer basket. Bake for 10 minutes. Turn and bake for an additional 5 to 10 minutes, or until browned and crisp on all sides. 5.Serve immediately.

Chapter 4
Snacks and Starters

Authentic Scotch Eggs

Prep time: 15 minutes | Cook time: 11 to 13 minutes | Serves 6

* 680 g bulk lean chicken or turkey banger
* 3 raw eggs, divided
* 100 g dried breadcrumbs,
* divided
* 65 g plain flour
* 6 hardboiled eggs, peeled
* Cooking oil spray

1. In a large bowl, combine the chicken banger, 1 raw egg, and 40 g of breadcrumbs and mix well. Divide the mixture into 6 pieces and flatten each into a long oval. 2. In a shallow dish, beat the remaining 2 raw eggs. 3. Place the flour in a small bowl. 4. Place the remaining 80 g of breadcrumbs in a second small bowl. 5. Roll each hardboiled egg in the flour and wrap one of the chicken banger pieces around each egg to encircle it completely. 6. One at a time, roll the encased eggs in the flour, dip in the beaten eggs, and finally dip in the breadcrumbs to coat. 7. Insert the crisper plate into the basket and the basket into the unit. Preheat the unit by selecting AIR FRY, setting the temperature to 190ºC, and setting the time to 3 minutes. Select START/STOP to begin. 8. Once the unit is preheated, spray the crisper plate with cooking oil. Place the eggs in a single layer into the basket and spray them with oil. 9. Select AIR FRY, set the temperature to 190ºC, and set the time to 13 minutes. Select START/STOP to begin. 10. After about 6 minutes, use tongs to turn the eggs and spray them with more oil. Resume cooking for 5 to 7 minutes more, or until the chicken is thoroughly cooked and the Scotch eggs are browned. 11. When the cooking is complete, serve warm.

Cheese Drops

Prep time: 15 minutes | Cook time: 10 minutes per batch | Serves 8

* 90 g plain flour
* ½ teaspoon rock salt
* ¼ teaspoon cayenne pepper
* ¼ teaspoon smoked paprika
* ¼ teaspoon black pepper
* a dash of garlic powder (optional)
* 57 g butter, softened
* 100 g grated extra mature cheddar cheese, at room temperature
* Olive oil spray

1. In a small bowl, combine the flour, salt, cayenne, paprika, pepper, and garlic powder, if using. 2. Using a food processor, cream the butter and cheese until smooth. Gently add the seasoned flour and process until the dough is well combined, smooth, and no longer sticky. (Or make the dough in a stand mixer fitted with the paddle attachment: Cream the butter and cheese at medium speed until smooth, then add the seasoned flour and beat at low speed until smooth.) 3. Divide the dough into 32 pieces of equal size. On a lightly floured surface, roll each piece into a small ball. 4. Spray the air fryer basket with oil spray. Arrange 16 cheese drops in the basket. Set the air

fryer to 160ºC for 10 minutes, or until drops are just starting to brown. Transfer to a a wire rack. Repeat with remaining dough, checking for degree of doneness at 8 minutes. 5. Cool the cheese drops completely on the a wire rack. Store in an airtight container until ready to serve, or up to 1 or 2 days.

Taco-Spiced Chickpeas

Prep time: 5 minutes | Cook time: 17 minutes | Serves 3

* Oil, for spraying
* 1 (439 g) tin chickpeas, drained
* 1 teaspoon chilli powder
* ½ teaspoon cumin
* powder
* ½ teaspoon salt
* ½ teaspoon garlic powder
* 2 teaspoons lime juice

1. Line the air fryer basket with baking paper and spray lightly with oil. Place the chickpeas in the prepared basket. 2. Air fry at 200ºC for 17 minutes, shaking or stirring the chickpeas and spraying lightly with oil every 5 to 7 minutes. 3. In a small bowl, mix together the chilli powder, cumin, salt, and garlic. 4. When 2 to 3 minutes of cooking time remain, sprinkle half of the seasoning mix over the chickpeas. Finish cooking. 5. Transfer the chickpeas to a medium-sized bowl and toss with the remaining seasoning mix and the lime juice. Serve immediately.

Onion Pakoras

Prep time: 30 minutes | Cook time: 10 minutes per batch | Serves 2

* two medium-sized brown or white onions, sliced (475 g)
* 30 g finely chopped fresh coriander
* 2 tablespoons mixed vegetables oil
* 1 tablespoon gram flour
* 1 tablespoon rice flour, or
* 2 tablespoons gram flour
* 1 teaspoon turmeric powder
* 1 teaspoon cumin seeds
* 1 teaspoon rock salt
* ½ teaspoon cayenne pepper
* mixed vegetables oil spray

1. In a large bowl, combine the onions, coriander, oil, gram flour, rice flour, turmeric, cumin seeds, salt, and cayenne. Stir to combine. Cover and let stand for 30 minutes or up to overnight. (This allows the onions to release moisture, creating a batter.) Mix well before using. 2. Spray the air fryer basket generously with mixed vegetables oil spray. Drop half of the batter in 6 heaped tablespoons into the basket. Set the air fryer to 180ºC for 8 minutes. Carefully turn the pakoras over and spray with oil spray. Set the air fryer for 2 minutes, or until the batter is fully cooked and crisp. 3. Repeat with remaining batter to make 6 more pakoras, checking at 6 minutes for degree of doneness. Serve hot.

Jalapeño Poppers

Prep time: 10 minutes | Cook time: 20 minutes | Serves 4

* Oil, for spraying
* 227 g soft white cheese
* 177 ml gluten-free breadcrumbs, divided
* 2 tablespoons chopped fresh parsley
* ½ teaspoon granulated garlic
* ½ teaspoon salt
* 10 red chillis, halved and seeded

1. Line the air fryer basket with parchment and spray lightly with oil. 2. In a medium bowl, mix together the soft white cheese, half of the breadcrumbs, the parsley, garlic, and salt. 3. Spoon the mixture into the jalapeño halves. Gently press the stuffed jalapeños in the remaining breadcrumbs. 4. Place the stuffed jalapeños in the prepared basket. 5. Air fry at 188°C for 20 minutes, or until the cheese is melted and the breadcrumbs are crisp and golden brown.

Prawns Egg Rolls

Prep time: 15 minutes | Cook time: 10 minutes per batch | Serves 4

* 1 tablespoon mixed vegetables oil
* ½ head green or savoy cabbage, finely shredded
* 90 g grated carrots
* 240 ml canned bean sprouts, drained
* 1 tablespoon soy sauce
* ½ teaspoon sugar
* 1 teaspoon sesame oil
* 60 ml hoisin sauce
* Freshly ground black pepper, to taste
* 454 g cooked prawns, diced
* 30 g spring onions
* 8 egg roll wrappers (or use spring roll pastry)
* mixed vegetables oil
* Duck sauce

1. Preheat a large sauté pan over medium-high heat. Add the oil and cook the cabbage, carrots and bean sprouts until they start to wilt, about 3 minutes. Add the soy sauce, sugar, sesame oil, hoisin sauce and black pepper. Sauté for a few more minutes. Stir in the prawns and spring onions and cook until the mixed vegetables are just tender. Transfer the mixture to a colander in a bowl to cool. Press or squeeze out any excess water from the filling so that you don't end up with soggy egg rolls. 2. Make the egg rolls: Place the egg roll wrappers on a flat surface with one of the points facing towards you so they look like diamonds. Dividing the filling evenly between the eight wrappers, spoon the mixture onto the centre of the egg roll wrappers. Spread the filling across the centre of the wrappers from the left corner to the right corner but leave 2 inches from each corner empty. Brush the empty sides of the wrapper with a little water. Fold the bottom corner tightly up over the filling, trying to avoid making any air pockets. Fold the left corner in toward the centre and then the right corner toward the centre. It should now look like an packet. Tightly roll the egg roll from the bottom to the top open corner. Press to seal the egg roll together, brushing with a little extra water if need be. Repeat this technique with all 8 egg rolls. 3. Preheat the air fryer to 190°C. 4. Spray or brush all sides of the egg rolls with mixed vegetables oil. Air fry four egg rolls at a time for 10 minutes, turning them over halfway through the cooking time. 5. Serve hot with duck sauce or your favourite dipping sauce.

Crispy Filo Artichoke Triangles

Prep time: 15 minutes | Cook time: 9 to 12 minutes | Makes 18 triangles

* 70 g Ricotta cheese
* 1 egg white
* 60 g minced and drained artichoke hearts
* 3 tablespoons grated mozzarella cheese cheese
* ½ teaspoon dried thyme
* 6 sheets frozen filo pastry, thawed
* 2 tablespoons melted butter

1. Preheat the air fryer to 200°C. 2. In a small bowl, combine the Ricotta cheese, egg white, artichoke hearts, mozzarella cheese cheese, and thyme, and mix well. 3. Cover the filo pastry with a damp kitchen towel while you work so it doesn't dry out. Using one sheet at a time, place on the work surface and cut into thirds lengthwise. 4. Put about 1½ teaspoons of the filling on each strip at the base. Fold the bottom right-hand tip of phyllo over the filling to meet the other side in a triangle, then continue folding in a triangle. Brush each triangle with butter to seal the edges. Repeat with the remaining phyllo dough and filling. 5. Place the triangles in the air fryer basket. Bake, 6 at a time, for about 3 to 4 minutes, or until the filo is golden and crisp. 6. Serve hot.

Rumaki

Prep time: 30 minutes | Cook time: 10 to 12 minutes per batch | Makes about 24 rumaki

* 283 g raw chicken livers
* 1 tin sliced water chestnuts, drained
* 60 ml low-salt teriyaki sauce
* 12 slices turkey bacon

1. Cut livers into 1½-inch pieces, trimming out tough veins as you slice. 2. Place livers, water chestnuts, and teriyaki sauce in small container with lid. If needed, add another tablespoon of teriyaki sauce to make sure livers are covered. Refrigerate for 1 hour. 3. When ready to cook, cut bacon slices in half crosswise. 4. Wrap 1 piece of liver and 1 slice of water chestnut in each bacon strip. Secure with a cocktail stick. 5. When you have wrapped half of the livers, place them in the air fryer basket in a single layer. 6. Air fry at 200°C for 10 to 12 minutes, until liver is done, and bacon is crispy. 7. While first batch cooks, wrap the remaining livers. Repeat step 6 to cook your second batch.

Lemon-Pepper Chicken Chicken Drumsticks

Prep time: 30 minutes | Cook time: 30 minutes | Serves 2

* 2 teaspoons freshly ground coarse black pepper
* 1 teaspoon baking powder
* ½ teaspoon garlic powder
* 4 chicken drumsticks (113 g each)
* Rock salt, to taste
* 1 lemon

1. In a small bowl, stir together the pepper, baking powder, and garlic powder. Place the drumsticks on a plate and sprinkle evenly with the baking powder mixture, turning the drumsticks so they're well coated. Let the drumsticks stand in the refrigerator for at least 1 hour or up to overnight. 2. Sprinkle the drumsticks with salt, then transfer them to the air fryer, standing them bone-side up and leaning against the wall of the air fryer basket. Air fry at 190ºC until fully cooked and crisp on the outside, about 30 minutes. 3. Transfer the drumsticks to a serving platter and finely grate the lemon zest over them while they're hot. Cut the lemon into wedges and serve with the warm drumsticks.

Baked Spanakopita Dip

Prep time: 10 minutes | Cook time: 15 minutes | Serves 2

* Olive oil cooking spray
* 3 tablespoons olive oil, divided
* 2 tablespoons minced white onion
* 2 garlic cloves, minced
* 100 g fresh spinach
* 113 g soft white cheese, softened
* 113 g feta cheese cheese,
* divided
* Zest of 1 lemon
* ¼ teaspoon ground nutmeg
* 1 teaspoon dried fresh dill
* ½ teaspoon salt
* Pitta chips, carrot sticks, or sliced bread for serving (optional)

1. Preheat the air fryer to 180ºC. Coat the inside of a 6-inch ramekin or baking dish with olive oil cooking spray. 2. In a large frying pan over medium heat, heat 1 tablespoon of the olive oil. Add the onion, then cook for 1 minute. 3. Add in the garlic and cook, stirring for 1 minute more. 4. Reduce the heat to low and mix in the spinach and water. Let this cook for 2 to 3 minutes, or until the spinach has wilted. Remove the frying pan from the heat. 5. In a medium-sized bowl, combine the soft white cheese, 57 g of the feta cheese, and the remaining 2 tablespoons of olive oil, along with the lemon zest, nutmeg, fresh dill, and salt. Mix until just combined. 6. Add the mixed vegetables to the cheese base and stir until combined. 7. Pour the dip mixture into the prepared ramekin and top with the remaining 57 g of feta cheese cheese. 8. Place the dip into the air fryer basket and cook for 10 minutes, or until heated through and bubbling. 9. Serve with pitta chips, carrot sticks, or sliced bread.

Sweet Potato Fries with Mayonnaise

Prep time: 5 minutes | Cook time: 20 minutes | Serves 2 to 3

* 1 large sweet potato (about 450 g), scrubbed
* 1 teaspoon mixed vegetables or rapeseed oil
* Salt, to taste
* Dipping Sauce:
* 60 ml light mayonnaise
* ½ teaspoon sriracha sauce
* 1 tablespoon spicy brown mustard
* 1 tablespoon sweet Thai chilli sauce

1. Preheat the air fryer to 90ºC. 2. On a flat work surface, cut the sweet potato into fry-shaped strips about ¼ inch wide and ¼ inch thick. You tin use a mandoline to slice the sweet potato quickly and uniformly. 3. In a medium-sized bowl, drizzle the sweet potato strips with the oil and toss well. 4. Transfer to the air fryer basket and air fry for 10 minutes, shaking the basket twice during cooking. 5. Remove the air fryer basket and sprinkle with the salt and toss to coat. 6. Increase the air fryer temperature to 200ºC and air fry for an additional 10 minutes, or until the fries are crispy and tender. Shake the basket a few times during cooking. 7. Meanwhile, whisk together all the ingredients for the sauce in a small bowl. 8. Remove the sweet potato fries from the basket to a plate and serve warm alongside the dipping sauce.

Polenta Fries with Chilli-Lime Mayo

Prep time: 10 minutes | Cook time: 28 minutes | Serves 4

* Polenta Fries:
* 2 teaspoons mixed vegetables or olive oil
* ¼ teaspoon paprika
* 450 g prepared polenta, cut into 3-inch × ½-inch strips
* Chilli-Lime Mayo:
* 120 ml mayonnaise
* 1 teaspoon chilli powder
* 1 teaspoon finely chopped fresh coriander
* ¼ teaspoon cumin powder
* Juice of ½ lime
* Salt and freshly ground black pepper, to taste

1. Preheat the air fryer to 200ºC. 2. Mix the oil and paprika in a bowl. Add the polenta strips and toss until evenly coated. 3. Transfer the polenta strips to the air fry basket and air fry for 28 minutes until the fries are golden, shaking the basket once during cooking. Season as desired with salt and pepper. 4. Meanwhile, whisk together all the ingredients for the chilli-lime mayo in a small bowl. 5. Remove the polenta fries from the air fryer to a plate and serve alongside the chilli-lime mayo as a dipping sauce.

Beef and Mango Skewers

Prep time: 10 minutes | Cook time: 4 to 7 minutes | Serves 4

* 340 g beef sirloin tip, cut into 1-inch cubes
* 2 tablespoons balsamic vinegar
* 1 tablespoon olive oil
* 1 tablespoon honey
* ½ teaspoon dried marjoram
* Pinch of salt
* Freshly ground black pepper, to taste
* 1 mango

1. Preheat the air fryer to 200ºC. 2. Put the beef cubes in a medium-sized bowl and add the balsamic vinegar, olive oil, honey, marjoram, salt, and pepper. Mix well, then massage the marinade into the beef with your hands. Set aside. 3. To prepare the mango, stand it on end and cut the skin off, using a sharp knife. Then carefully cut around the oval pit to remove the flesh. Cut the mango into 1-inch cubes. 4. Thread metal skewers alternating with three beef cubes and two mango cubes. 5. Roast the skewers in the air fryer basket for 4 to 7 minutes, or until the beef is browned and at least 63ºC. 6. Serve hot.

Herbed Green Lentil Rice Balls

Prep time: 5 minutes | Cook time: 11 minutes | Serves 6

* 120 ml cooked green lentils
* 2 garlic cloves, minced
* ¼ white onion, minced
* 60 ml parsley leaves
* 5 basil leaves
* 235 ml cooked brown rice
* 1 tablespoon lemon juice
* 1 tablespoon olive oil
* ½ teaspoon salt

1. Preheat the air fryer to 192ºC. 2. In a food processor, pulse the cooked lentils with the garlic, onion, parsley, and basil until mostly smooth. (You will want some bits of lentils in the mixture.) Pour the lentil mixture into a large bowl, and stir in brown rice, lemon juice, olive oil, and salt. Stir until well combined. 3. Form the rice mixture into 1-inch balls. 4. Place the rice balls in a single layer in the air fryer basket, making sure that they don't touch each other. 5. Fry for 6 minutes. 6. Turn the rice balls and then fry for an additional 4 to 5 minutes, or until browned on all sides.

Peppery Chicken Meatballs

Prep time: 5 minutes | Cook time: 13 to 20 minutes | Makes 16 meatballs

* 2 teaspoons olive oil
* 35 g minced onion
* 35 g minced red pepper
* 2 vanilla wafers, crushed
* 1 egg white
* ½ teaspoon dried thyme
* 230 g minced chicken breast

1. Preheat the air fryer to 188ºC. 2. In a baking pan, mix the olive oil, onion, and red pepper. Put the pan in the air fryer. Air fry for 3 to 5 minutes, or until the mixed vegetables are tender. 3. In a medium-sized bowl, mix the cooked mixed vegetables, crushed wafers, egg white, and thyme until well combined 4. Mix in the chicken, gently but thoroughly, until everything is combined. 5. Form the mixture into 16 meatballs and place them in the air fryer basket. Air fry for 10 to 15 minutes, or until the meatballs reach an internal temperature of 70ºC on a meat thermometer. 6. Serve immediately.

Crispy Potato Chips with Lemony Cream Dip

Prep time: 20 minutes | Cook time: 15 minutes | Serves 2 to 4

* 2 large russet or Maris Piper potatoes, sliced into ⅛-inch slices, rinsed
* Sea salt and freshly ground black pepper, to taste
* Cooking spray
* Lemony Cream Dip:
* 120 ml sour cream
* ¼ teaspoon lemon juice
* 2 spring onions, white part only, minced
* 1 tablespoon olive oil
* ¼ teaspoon salt
* Freshly ground black pepper, to taste

1. Soak the potato slices in water for 10 minutes, then pat dry with paper towels 2. Preheat the air fryer to 150ºC 3. Transfer the potato slices in the preheated air fryer 4. Spritz the slices with cooking spray 5. You may need to work in batches to avoid overcrowding 6. Air fry for 15 minutes or until crispy and golden brown 7. Shake the basket periodically 8. Sprinkle with salt and ground black pepper in the last minute 9. Meanwhile, combine the ingredients for the dip in a small bowl 10. Stir to mix well 11. Serve the potato chips immediately with the dip.

Roasted Mushrooms with Garlic

Prep time: 3 minutes | Cook time: 22 to 27 minutes | Serves 4

* 16 garlic cloves, peeled
* 2 teaspoons olive oil, divided
* 16 button mushrooms
* ½ teaspoon dried marjoram
* ⅛ teaspoon freshly ground black pepper
* 1 tablespoon white wine or low-salt mixed vegetables broth

1. In a baking pan, mix the garlic with 1 teaspoon of olive oil. Roast in the air fryer at 180ºC for 12 minutes. 2. Add the mushrooms, marjoram, and pepper. Stir to coat. Drizzle with the remaining 1 teaspoon of olive oil and the white wine. 3. Return to the air fryer and roast for 10 to 15 minutes more, or until the mushrooms and garlic cloves are tender. Serve.

Mozzarella Cheese Arancini

Prep time: 5 minutes | Cook time: 8 to 11 minutes | Makes 16 arancini

* 250 g cooked rice, cooled
* 2 eggs, beaten
* 90 g panko breadcrumbs, divided
* 45 g grated Parmesan cheese
* 2 tablespoons minced fresh basil
* 16¾-inch cubes mozzarella cheese cheese
* 2 tablespoons olive oil

1. Preheat the air fryer to 200°C. 2. In a medium-sized bowl, combine the rice, eggs, 120 ml of the breadcrumbs, Parmesan cheese, and basil. Form this mixture into 16 1½-inch balls. 3. Poke a hole in each of the balls with your finger and insert a mozzarella cheese cube. Form the rice mixture firmly around the cheese. 4. On a shallow plate, combine the remaining 100 g of the breadcrumbs with the olive oil and mix well. Roll the rice balls in the breadcrumbs to coat. 5. Air fry the arancini in batches for 8 to 11 minutes or until golden. 6. Serve hot.

Honey-Mustard Chicken Wings

Prep time: 10 minutes | Cook time: 24 minutes | Serves 2

* 907 g chicken wings
* Salt and freshly ground black pepper, to taste
* 2 tablespoons butter
* 60 ml honey
* 60 g spicy brown mustard
* Pinch ground cayenne pepper
* 2 teaspoons Worcestershire sauce

1. Prepare the chicken wings by cutting off the wing tips and discarding (or freezing for chicken stock). Divide the chicken drumettes from the chicken wingettes by cutting through the joint. Place the chicken wing pieces in a large bowl. 2. Preheat the air fryer to 200°C. 3. Season the wings with salt and freshly ground black pepper and air fry the wings in two batches for 10 minutes per batch, shaking the basket halfway through the cooking process. 4. While the wings are air frying, combine the remaining ingredients in a small saucepan over low heat. 5. When both batches are done, toss all the wings with the honey-mustard sauce and toss them all back into the basket for another 4 minutes to heat through and finish cooking. Give the basket a good shake part way through the cooking process to redistribute the wings. Remove the wings from the air fryer and serve.

Crispy Mozzarella Cheese Sticks

Prep time: 8 minutes | Cook time: 5 minutes | Serves 4

* 65 g plain flour
* 1 egg, beaten
* 25 g panko breadcrumbs
* 30 g grated Parmesan cheese
* 1 teaspoon Italian seasoning
* ½ teaspoon garlic salt
* 6 mozzarella cheese sticks, halved crosswise
* Olive oil spray

1. Put the flour in a small bowl. 2. Put the beaten egg in another small bowl. 3. In a medium-sized bowl, stir together the panko, Parmesan cheese, Italian seasoning, and garlic salt. 4. Roll a mozzarella cheese-stick half in the flour, dip it into the egg, and then roll it in the panko mixture to coat. Press the coating lightly to make sure the breadcrumbs stick to the cheese. Repeat with the remaining 11 mozzarella cheese sticks. 5. Insert the crisper plate into the basket and the basket into the unit. Preheat the unit by selecting AIR FRY, setting the temperature to 200°C, and setting the time to 3 minutes. Select START/STOP to begin. 6. Once the unit is preheated, spray the crisper plate with olive oil and place a baking paper paper liner in the basket. Place the mozzarella cheese sticks into the basket and lightly spray them with olive oil. 7. Select AIR FRY, set the temperature to 200°C, and set the time to 5 minutes. Select START/STOP to begin. 8. When the cooking is complete, the mozzarella cheese sticks should be golden and crispy. Let the sticks stand for 1 minute before transferring them to a serving plate. Serve warm.

Chapter 5
Beef, Pork, and Lamb

Greek Lamb Rack

Prep time: 5 minutes | Cook time: 10 minutes | Serves 4

* 60 g freshly squeezed lemon juice
* 1 teaspoon oregano
* 2 teaspoons minced fresh rosemary
* 1 teaspoon minced fresh thyme
* 2 tablespoons minced
* garlic
* Salt and freshly ground black pepper, to taste
* 2 to 4 tablespoons olive oil
* 1 lamb rib rack (7 to 8 ribs)

1. Preheat the air fryer to 180°C. 2. In a small mixing bowl, combine the lemon juice, oregano, rosemary, thyme, garlic, salt, pepper, and olive oil and mix well. 3. Rub the mixture over the lamb, covering all the meat. Put the rack of lamb in the air fryer. Roast for 10 minutes. Flip the rack halfway through. 4. After 10 minutes, measure the internal temperature of the rack of lamb reaches at least 64°C. 5. Serve immediately.

Panko Pork Chops

Prep time: 10 minutes | Cook time: 12 minutes | Serves 4

* 4 boneless pork chops, excess fat trimmed
* ¼ teaspoon salt
* 2 eggs
* 130 g panko bread crumbs
* 3 tablespoons grated Parmesan cheese
* 1½ teaspoons paprika
* ½ teaspoon granulated garlic
* ½ teaspoon onion granules
* 1 teaspoon chilli powder
* ¼ teaspoon freshly ground black pepper
* Olive oil spray

1. Sprinkle the pork chops with salt on both sides and let them sit while you prepare the seasonings and egg wash. 2. In a shallow medium bowl, beat the eggs. 3. In another shallow medium bowl, stir together the panko, Parmesan cheese, paprika, granulated garlic, onion granules, chilli powder, and pepper. 4. Dip the pork chops in the egg and in the panko mixture to coat. Firmly press the crumbs onto the chops. 5. Insert the crisper plate into the basket and the basket into the unit. Preheat the unit by selecting AIR ROAST, setting the temperature to 200°C, and setting the time to 3 minutes. Select START/STOP to begin. 6. Once the unit is preheated, spray the crisper plate with olive oil. Place the pork chops into the basket and spray them with olive oil. 7. Select AIR ROAST, set the temperature to 200°C, and set the time to 12 minutes. Select START/STOP to begin. 8. After 6 minutes, flip the pork chops and spray them with more olive oil. Resume cooking. 9. When the cooking is complete, the chops should be golden and crispy and a food thermometer should register 64°C. Serve immediately.

Five-Spice Pork Belly

Prep time: 10 minutes | Cook time: 17 minutes | Serves 4

* 450 g unsalted pork belly
* 2 teaspoons Chinese five-spice powder
* Sauce:
* 1 tablespoon coconut oil
* 1 (1-inch) piece fresh ginger, peeled and grated
* 2 cloves garlic, minced
* 120 ml beef or chicken stock
* ¼ to 120 ml liquid or powdered sweetener
* 3 tablespoons wheat-free tamari
* 1 spring onion, sliced, plus more for garnish

1. Spray the air fryer basket with avocado oil. Preheat the air fryer to 200°C. 2. Cut the pork belly into ½-inch-thick slices and season well on all sides with the five-spice powder. Place the slices in a single layer in the air fryer basket (if you're using a smaller air fryer, work in batches if necessary) and cook for 8 minutes, or until cooked to your liking, flipping halfway through. 3. While the pork belly cooks, make the sauce: Heat the coconut oil in a small saucepan over medium heat. Add the ginger and garlic and sauté for 1 minute, or until fragrant. Add the stock, sweetener, and tamari and simmer for 10 to 15 minutes, until thickened. Add the spring onion and cook for another minute, until the spring onion is softened. Taste and adjust the seasoning to your liking. 4. Transfer the pork belly to a large bowl. Pour the sauce over the pork belly and coat well. Place the pork belly slices on a serving platter and garnish with sliced spring onions. 5. Best served fresh. Store leftovers in an airtight container in the fridge for up to 4 days. Reheat in a preheated 200°C air fryer for 3 minutes, or until heated through.

Air Fried Crispy Venison

Prep time: 10 minutes | Cook time: 20 minutes | Serves 4

* 2 eggs
* 60 ml milk
* 120 g whole wheat flour
* ½ teaspoon salt
* ¼ teaspoon ground black
* pepper
* 450 g venison backstrap/striploin, sliced
* Cooking spray

1. Preheat the air fryer to 180°C and spritz with cooking spray. 2. Whisk the eggs with milk in a large bowl. Combine the flour with salt and ground black pepper in a shallow dish. 3. Dredge the venison in the flour first, then into the egg mixture. Shake the excess off and roll the venison back over the flour to coat well. 4. Arrange half of the venison in the preheated air fryer and spritz with cooking spray. 5. Air fry for 10 minutes or until the internal temperature of the venison reaches at least 64°C for medium rare. Flip the venison halfway through. Repeat with remaining venison. 6. Serve immediately.

Chapter 5 Beef, Pork, and Lamb 23

Bacon and Cheese Stuffed Pork Chops

Prep time: 10 minutes | Cook time: 12 minutes | Serves 4

* 15 g plain pork scratchings, finely crushed
* 120 g shredded sharp Cheddar cheese
* 4 slices cooked bacon, crumbled
* 4 (110 g) boneless pork chops
* ½ teaspoon salt
* ¼ teaspoon ground black pepper

1. In a small bowl, mix pork scratchings, Cheddar, and bacon. 2. Make a 3-inch slit in the side of each pork chop and stuff with ¼ pork rind mixture. Sprinkle each side of pork chops with salt and pepper. 3. Place pork chops into ungreased air fryer basket, stuffed side up. Adjust the temperature to 200°C and air fry for 12 minutes. Pork chops will be browned and have an internal temperature of at least 64°C when done. Serve warm.

Simple Beef Mince with Courgette

Prep time: 5 minutes | Cook time: 12 minutes | Serves 4

* 680 g beef mince
* 450 g chopped courgette
* 2 tablespoons extra-virgin olive oil
* 1 teaspoon dried oregano
* 1 teaspoon dried basil
* 1 teaspoon dried rosemary
* 2 tablespoons fresh chives, chopped

1. Preheat the air fryer to 200°C. 2. In a large bowl, combine all the ingredients, except for the chives, until well blended. 3. Place the beef and courgette mixture in the baking tray. Air fry for 12 minutes, or until the beef is browned and the courgette is tender. 4. Divide the beef and courgette mixture among four serving dishes. Top with fresh chives and serve hot.

Cheese Crusted Chops

Prep time: 10 minutes | Cook time: 12 minutes | Serves 4 to 6

* ¼ teaspoon pepper
* ½ teaspoons salt
* 4 to 6 thick boneless pork chops
* 235 g pork scratching crumbs
* ¼ teaspoon chilli powder
* ½ teaspoons onion granules
* 1 teaspoon smoked paprika
* 2 beaten eggs
* 3 tablespoons grated Parmesan cheese
* Cooking spray

1. Preheat the air fryer to 210°C. 2. Rub the pepper and salt on both sides of pork chops. 3. In a food processor, pulse pork scratchings into crumbs. Mix crumbs with chilli powder, onion granules, and paprika in a bowl. 4. Beat eggs in another bowl. 5. Dip pork chops into eggs then into pork scratchings crumb mixture. 6. Spritz the air fryer basket with cooking spray and add pork chops to the basket. 7. Air fry for 12 minutes. 8. Serve garnished with the Parmesan cheese.

Mojito Lamb Chops

Prep time: 30 minutes | Cook time: 5 minutes | Serves 2

* Marinade:
* 2 teaspoons grated lime zest
* 120 ml lime juice
* 60 ml avocado oil
* 60 g chopped fresh mint leaves
* 4 cloves garlic, roughly chopped
* 2 teaspoons fine sea salt
* ½ teaspoon ground black pepper
* 4 (1-inch-thick) lamb chops
* Sprigs of fresh mint, for garnish (optional)
* Lime slices, for serving (optional)

1. Make the marinade: Place all the ingredients for the marinade in a food processor or blender and purée until mostly smooth with a few small chunks. Transfer half of the marinade to a shallow dish and set the other half aside for serving. Add the lamb to the shallow dish, cover, and place in the refrigerator to marinate for at least 2 hours or overnight. 2. Spray the air fryer basket with avocado oil. Preheat the air fryer to 200°C. 3. Remove the chops from the marinade and place them in the air fryer basket. Air fry for 5 minutes, or until the internal temperature reaches 64°C for medium doneness. 4. Allow the chops to rest for 10 minutes before serving with the rest of the marinade as a sauce. Garnish with fresh mint leaves and serve with lime slices, if desired. Best served fresh.

Pigs in a Blanket

Prep time: 10 minutes | Cook time: 7 minutes | Serves 2

* 120 g shredded Mozzarella cheese
* 2 tablespoons blanched finely ground almond flour
* 30 g full-fat cream cheese
* 2 (110 g) beef smoked banger, cut in two
* ½ teaspoon sesame seeds

1. Place Mozzarella, almond flour, and cream cheese in a large microwave-safe bowl. Microwave for 45 seconds and stir until smooth. Roll dough into a ball and cut in half. 2. Press each half out into a 4 × 5-inch rectangle. Roll one banger up in each dough half and press seams closed. Sprinkle the top with sesame seeds. 3. Place each wrapped banger into the air fryer basket. 4. Adjust the temperature to 200°C and air fry for 7 minutes. 5. The outside will be golden when completely cooked. Serve immediately.

Herbed Beef

Prep time: 5 minutes | Cook time: 22 minutes | Serves 6

* 1 teaspoon dried dill
* 1 teaspoon dried thyme
* 1 teaspoon garlic powder
* 900 g beef steak
* 3 tablespoons butter

1. Preheat the air fryer to 180ºC. 2. Combine the dill, thyme, and garlic powder in a small bowl, and massage into the steak. 3. Air fry the steak in the air fryer for 20 minutes, then remove, shred, and return to the air fryer. 4. Add the butter and air fry the shredded steak for a further 2 minutes at 190ºC. Make sure the beef is coated in the butter before serving.

Green Pepper Cheeseburgers

Prep time: 5 minutes | Cook time: 30 minutes | Serves 4

* 2 green peppers
* 680 g 85% lean beef mince
* 1 clove garlic, minced
* 1 teaspoon salt
* ½ teaspoon freshly ground black pepper
* 4 slices Cheddar cheese (about 85 g)
* 4 large lettuce leaves

1. Preheat the air fryer to 200ºC. 2. Arrange the peppers in the basket of the air fryer. Pausing halfway through the cooking time to turn the peppers, air fry for 20 minutes, or until they are softened and beginning to char. Transfer the peppers to a large bowl and cover with a plate. When cool enough to handle, peel off the skin, remove the seeds and stems, and slice into strips. Set aside. 3. Meanwhile, in a large bowl, combine the beef with the garlic, salt, and pepper. Shape the beef into 4 patties. 4. Lower the heat on the air fryer to 180ºC. Arrange the burgers in a single layer in the basket of the air fryer. Pausing halfway through the cooking time to turn the burgers, air fry for 10 minutes, or until a thermometer inserted into the thickest part registers 72ºC. 5. Top the burgers with the cheese slices and continue baking for a minute or two, just until the cheese has melted. Serve the burgers on a lettuce leaf topped with the roasted peppers.

Peppercorn-Crusted Beef Fillet

Prep time: 10 minutes | Cook time: 25 minutes | Serves 6

* 2 tablespoons salted melted butter
* 2 teaspoons minced roasted garlic
* 3 tablespoons ground 4-peppercorn blend
* 1 (900 g) beef fillet, trimmed of visible fat

1. In a small bowl, mix the butter and roasted garlic. Brush it over the beef fillet. 2. Place the ground peppercorns onto a plate and roll the fillet through them, creating a crust. Place fillet into the air fryer basket. 3. Adjust the temperature to 200ºC and roast for 25 minutes. 4. Turn the fillet halfway through the cooking time. 5. Allow meat to rest 10 minutes before slicing.

Honey-Baked Pork Loin

Prep time: 30 minutes | Cook time: 22 to 25 minutes | Serves 6

* 60 ml honey
* 60 g freshly squeezed lemon juice
* 2 tablespoons soy sauce
* 1 teaspoon garlic powder
* 1 (900 g) pork loin
* 2 tablespoons vegetable oil

1. In a medium bowl, whisk together the honey, lemon juice, soy sauce, and garlic powder. Reserve half of the mixture for basting during cooking. 2. Cut 5 slits in the pork loin and transfer it to a resealable bag. Add the remaining honey mixture. Seal the bag and refrigerate to marinate for at least 2 hours. 3. Preheat the air fryer to 200ºC. Line the air fryer basket with parchment paper. 4. Remove the pork from the marinade, and place it on the parchment. Spritz with oil, then baste with the reserved marinade. 5. Cook for 15 minutes. Flip the pork, baste with more marinade and spritz with oil again. Cook for 7 to 10 minutes more until the internal temperature reaches 64ºC. Let rest for 5 minutes before serving.

Marinated Steak Tips with Mushrooms

Prep time: 30 minutes | Cook time: 10 minutes | Serves 4

* 680 g rump steak, trimmed and cut into 1-inch pieces
* 230 g brown mushrooms, halved
* 60 ml Worcestershire sauce
* 1 tablespoon Dijon
* mustard
* 1 tablespoon olive oil
* 1 teaspoon paprika
* 1 teaspoon crushed red pepper flakes
* 2 tablespoons chopped fresh parsley (optional)

1. Place the beef and mushrooms in a gallon-size resealable bag. In a small bowl, whisk together the Worcestershire, mustard, olive oil, paprika, and red pepper flakes. Pour the marinade into the bag and massage gently to ensure the beef and mushrooms are evenly coated. Seal the bag and refrigerate for at least 4 hours, preferably overnight. Remove from the refrigerator 30 minutes before cooking. 2. Preheat the air fryer to 200ºC. 3. Drain and discard the marinade. Arrange the steak and mushrooms in the air fryer basket. Air fry for 10 minutes, pausing halfway through the baking time to shake the basket. Transfer to a serving plate and top with the parsley, if desired.

Chapter 5   Beef, Pork, and Lamb   25

Pork Milanese

Prep time: 10 minutes | Cook time: 12 minutes | Serves 4

* 4 (1-inch) boneless pork chops
* Fine sea salt and ground black pepper, to taste
* 2 large eggs
* 180 g pre-grated Parmesan cheese
* Chopped fresh parsley, for garnish
* Lemon slices, for serving

1. Spray the air fryer basket with avocado oil. Preheat the air fryer to 200°C. 2. Place the pork chops between 2 sheets of cling film and pound them with the flat side of a meat tenderizer until they're ¼ inch thick. Lightly season both sides of the chops with salt and pepper. 3. Lightly beat the eggs in a shallow bowl. Divide the Parmesan cheese evenly between 2 bowls and set the bowls in this order: Parmesan, eggs, Parmesan. Dredge a chop in the first bowl of Parmesan, then dip it in the eggs, and then dredge it again in the second bowl of Parmesan, making sure both sides and all edges are well coated. Repeat with the remaining chops. 4. Place the chops in the air fryer basket and air fry for 12 minutes, or until the internal temperature reaches 64°C, flipping halfway through. 5. Garnish with fresh parsley and serve immediately with lemon slices. Store leftovers in an airtight container in the refrigerator for up to 3 days. Reheat in a preheated 200°C air fryer for 5 minutes, or until warmed through.

Spicy Lamb Sirloin Chops

Prep time: 30 minutes | Cook time: 15 minutes | Serves 4

* ½ brown onion, coarsely chopped
* 4 coin-size slices peeled fresh ginger
* 5 garlic cloves
* 1 teaspoon garam masala
* 1 teaspoon ground fennel
* 1 teaspoon ground cinnamon
* 1 teaspoon ground turmeric
* ½ to 1 teaspoon cayenne pepper
* ½ teaspoon ground cardamom
* 1 teaspoon coarse or flaky salt
* 450 g lamb sirloin chops

1. In a blender, combine the onion, ginger, garlic, garam masala, fennel, cinnamon, turmeric, cayenne, cardamom, and salt. Pulse until the onion is finely minced and the mixture forms a thick paste, 3 to 4 minutes. 2. Place the lamb chops in a large bowl. Slash the meat and fat with a sharp knife several times to allow the marinade to penetrate better. Add the spice paste to the bowl and toss the lamb to coat. Marinate at room temperature for 30 minutes or cover and refrigerate for up to 24 hours. 3. Place the lamb chops in a single layer in the air fryer basket. Set the air fryer to 160°C for 15 minutes, turning the chops halfway through the cooking time. Use a meat thermometer to ensure the lamb has reached an internal temperature of 64°C (medium-rare).

Chorizo and Beef Burger

Prep time: 10 minutes | Cook time: 15 minutes | Serves 4

* 340 g 80/20 beef mince
* 110 g Mexican-style chorizo crumb
* 60 g chopped onion
* 5 slices pickled jalapeños,
* chopped
* 2 teaspoons chilli powder
* 1 teaspoon minced garlic
* ¼ teaspoon cumin

1. In a large bowl, mix all ingredients. Divide the mixture into four sections and form them into burger patties. 2. Place burger patties into the air fryer basket, working in batches if necessary. 3. Adjust the temperature to 190°C and air fry for 15 minutes. 4. Flip the patties halfway through the cooking time. Serve warm.

Lamb and Cucumber Burgers

Prep time: 8 minutes | Cook time: 15 to 18 minutes | Serves 4

* 1 teaspoon ground ginger
* ½ teaspoon ground coriander
* ¼ teaspoon freshly ground white pepper
* ½ teaspoon ground cinnamon
* ½ teaspoon dried oregano
* ¼ teaspoon ground allspice
* ¼ teaspoon ground
* turmeric
* 120 ml low-fat plain Greek yoghurt
* 450 g lamb mince
* 1 teaspoon garlic paste
* ¼ teaspoon salt
* ¼ teaspoon freshly ground black pepper
* Cooking oil spray
* 4 hamburger buns
* ½ cucumber, thinly sliced

1. In a small bowl, stir together the ginger, coriander, white pepper, cinnamon, oregano, allspice, and turmeric. 2. Put the yoghurt in a small bowl and add half the spice mixture. Mix well and refrigerate. 3. Insert the crisper plate into the basket and the basket into the unit. Preheat the unit by selecting AIR FRY, setting the temperature to 180°C, and setting the time to 3 minutes. Select START/STOP to begin. 4. In a large bowl, combine the lamb, garlic paste, remaining spice mix, salt, and pepper. Gently but thoroughly mix the ingredients with your hands. Form the meat into 4 patties. 5. Once the unit is preheated, spray the crisper plate with cooking oil, and place the patties into the basket. 6. Select AIR FRY, set the temperature to 180°C, and set the time to 18 minutes. Select START/STOP to begin. 7. After 15 minutes, check the burgers. If a food thermometer inserted into the burgers registers 72°C, the burgers are done. If not, resume cooking. 8. When the cooking is complete, assemble the burgers on the buns with cucumber slices and a dollop of the yoghurt dip.

Pork Bulgogi

Prep time: 30 minutes | Cook time: 15 minutes | Serves 4

* 1 onion, thinly sliced
* 2 tablespoons gochujang (Korean red chilli paste)
* 1 tablespoon minced fresh ginger
* 1 tablespoon minced garlic
* 1 tablespoon soy sauce
* 1 tablespoon Shaoxing wine (rice cooking wine)
* 1 tablespoon toasted sesame oil
* 1 teaspoon sugar
* ¼ to 1 teaspoon cayenne pepper or gochugaru (Korean ground red pepper)
* 450 g boneless pork shoulder, cut into ½-inch-thick slices
* 1 tablespoon sesame seeds
* 60 g sliced spring onionspring onions

1. In a large bowl, combine the onion, gochujang, ginger, garlic, soy sauce, wine, sesame oil, sugar, and cayenne. Add the pork and toss to coat. Marinate at room temperature for 30 minutes, or cover and refrigerate for up to 24 hours. 2. Arrange the pork and onion slices in the air fryer basket; discard the marinade. Set the air fryer to 200°C for 15 minutes, turning the pork halfway through the cooking time. 3. Arrange the pork on a serving platter. Sprinkle with the sesame seeds and spring onionspring onions and serve.

Indian Mint and Chile Kebabs

Prep time: 30 minutes | Cook time: 15 minutes | Serves 4

* 450 g lamb mince
* 120 g finely minced onion
* 60 g chopped fresh mint
* 60 g chopped fresh coriander
* 1 tablespoon minced garlic
* ½ teaspoon ground
* turmeric
* ½ teaspoon cayenne pepper
* ¼ teaspoon ground cardamom
* ¼ teaspoon ground cinnamon
* 1 teaspoon coarse or flaky salt

1. In the bowl of a stand mixer fitted with the paddle attachment, combine the lamb, onion, mint, coriander, garlic, turmeric, cayenne, cardamom, cinnamon, and salt. Mix on low speed until you have a sticky mess of spiced meat. If you have time, let the mixture stand at room temperature for 30 minutes (or cover and refrigerate for up to a day or two, until you're ready to make the kebabs). 2. Divide the meat into eight equal portions. Form each into a long banger shape. Place the kebabs in a single layer in the air fryer basket. Set the air fryer to 180°C for 10 minutes. Increase the air fryer temperature to 200°C and cook for 3 to 4 minutes more to brown the kebabs. Use a meat thermometer to ensure the kebabs have reached an internal temperature of 72°C (medium).

Bacon Wrapped Pork with Apple Gravy

Prep time: 10 minutes | Cook time: 25 minutes | Serves 4

* Pork:
* 1 tablespoons Dijon mustard
* 1 pork tenderloin
* 3 strips bacon
* Apple Gravy:
* 3 tablespoons ghee, divided
* 1 small shallot, chopped
* 2 apples
* 1 tablespoon almond flour
* 235 ml vegetable stock
* ½ teaspoon Dijon mustard

1. Preheat the air fryer to 180°C. 2. Spread Dijon mustard all over tenderloin and wrap with strips of bacon. 3. Put into air fryer and air fry for 12 minutes. Use a meat thermometer to check for doneness. 4. To make sauce, heat 1 tablespoons of ghee in a pan and add shallots. Cook for 1 minute. 5. Then add apples, cooking for 4 minutes until softened. 6. Add flour and 2 tablespoons of ghee to make a roux. Add stock and mustard, stirring well to combine. 7. When sauce starts to bubble, add 235 g of sautéed apples, cooking until sauce thickens. 8. Once pork tenderloin is cooked, allow to sit 8 minutes to rest before slicing. 9. Serve topped with apple gravy.

Pork Kebab with Yoghurt Sauce

Prep time: 25 minutes | Cook time: 12 minutes | Serves 4

* 2 teaspoons olive oil
* 230 g pork mince
* 230 g beef mince
* 1 egg, whisked
* Sea salt and ground black pepper, to taste
* 1 teaspoon paprika
* 2 garlic cloves, minced
* 1 teaspoon dried marjoram
* 1 teaspoon mustard seeds
* ½ teaspoon celery salt
* Yoghurt Sauce:
* 2 tablespoons olive oil
* 2 tablespoons fresh lemon juice
* Sea salt, to taste
* ¼ teaspoon red pepper flakes, crushed
* 120 ml full-fat yoghurt
* 1 teaspoon dried dill

1. Spritz the sides and bottom of the air fryer basket with 2 teaspoons of olive oil. 2. In a mixing dish, thoroughly combine the pork, beef, egg, salt, black pepper, paprika, garlic, marjoram, mustard seeds, and celery salt. 3. Form the mixture into kebabs and transfer them to the greased basket. Cook at 190°C for 11 to 12 minutes, turning them over once or twice. In the meantime, mix all the sauce ingredients and place in the refrigerator until ready to serve. Serve the pork kebabs with the yoghurt sauce on the side. Enjoy!

Southern Chilli

Prep time: 20 minutes | Cook time: 25 minutes | Serves 4

* 450 g beef mince (85% lean)
* 235 g minced onion
* 1 (794 g) tin tomato purée
* 1 (425 g) tin diced tomatoes
* 1 (425 g) tin red kidney beans, rinsed and drained
* 60 g Chili seasoning

1. Preheat the air fryer to 200ºC. 2. In a baking tray, mix the mince and onion. Place the pan in the air fryer. 3. Cook for 4 minutes. Stir and cook for 4 minutes more until browned. Remove the pan from the fryer. Drain the meat and transfer to a large bowl. 4. Reduce the air fryer temperature to 180ºC. 5. To the bowl with the meat, add in the tomato purée, diced tomatoes, kidney beans, and Chili seasoning. Mix well. Pour the mixture into the baking tray. 6. Cook for 25 minutes, stirring every 10 minutes, until thickened.

Smoky Pork Tenderloin

Prep time: 5 minutes | Cook time: 19 to 22 minutes | Serves 6

* 680 g pork tenderloin
* 1 tablespoon avocado oil
* 1 teaspoon chilli powder
* 1 teaspoon smoked paprika
* 1 teaspoon garlic powder
* 1 teaspoon sea salt
* 1 teaspoon freshly ground black pepper

1. Pierce the tenderloin all over with a fork and rub the oil all over the meat. 2. In a small dish, stir together the chilli powder, smoked paprika, garlic powder, salt, and pepper. 3. Rub the spice mixture all over the tenderloin. 4. Set the air fryer to 200ºC. Place the pork in the air fryer basket and air fry for 10 minutes. Flip the tenderloin and cook for 9 to 12 minutes more, until an instant-read thermometer reads at least 64ºC. 5. Allow the tenderloin to rest for 5 minutes, then slice and serve.

Ham with Sweet Potatoes

Prep time: 20 minutes | Cook time: 15 to 17 minutes | Serves 4

* 235 g freshly squeezed orange juice
* 96 g packed light brown sugar
* 1 tablespoon Dijon mustard
* ½ teaspoon salt
* ½ teaspoon freshly ground black pepper
* 3 sweet potatoes, cut into small wedges
* 2 gammon steaks (230 g each), halved
* 1 to 2 tablespoons oil

1. In a large bowl, whisk the orange juice, brown sugar, Dijon, salt, and pepper until blended. Toss the sweet potato wedges with the brown sugar mixture. 2. Preheat the air fryer to 200ºC. Line the air fryer basket with parchment paper and spritz with oil. 3. Place the sweet potato wedges on the parchment. 4. Cook for 10 minutes. 5. Place gammon steaks on top of the sweet potatoes and brush everything with more of the orange juice mixture. 6. Cook for 3 minutes. Flip the gammon and cook or 2 to 4 minutes more until the sweet potatoes are soft and the glaze has thickened. Cut the gammon steaks in half to serve.

Sweet and Spicy Country-Style Ribs

Prep time: 10 minutes | Cook time: 25 minutes | Serves 4

* 2 tablespoons brown sugar
* 2 tablespoons smoked paprika
* 1 teaspoon garlic powder
* 1 teaspoon onion granules
* 1 teaspoon mustard powder
* 1 teaspoon ground cumin
* 1 teaspoon coarse or flaky salt
* 1 teaspoon black pepper
* ¼ to ½ teaspoon cayenne pepper
* 680 g boneless pork steaks
* 235 ml barbecue sauce

1. In a small bowl, stir together the brown sugar, paprika, garlic powder, onion granules, mustard powder, cumin, salt, black pepper, and cayenne. Mix until well combined. 2. Pat the ribs dry with a paper towel. Generously sprinkle the rub evenly over both sides of the ribs and rub in with your fingers. 3. Place the ribs in the air fryer basket. Set the air fryer to 180ºC for 15 minutes. Turn the ribs and brush with 120 ml of the barbecue sauce. Cook for an additional 10 minutes. Use a meat thermometer to ensure the pork has reached an internal temperature of 64ºC. 4. Serve with remaining barbecue sauce.

Super Bacon with Meat

Prep time: 5 minutes | Cook time: 1 hour | Serves 4

* 30 slices thick-cut bacon
* 110 g Cheddar cheese, shredded
* 340 g steak
* 280 g pork banger meat
* Salt and ground black pepper, to taste

1. Preheat the air fryer to 200ºC. 2. Lay out 30 slices of bacon in a woven pattern and bake for 20 minutes until crisp. Put the cheese in the center of the bacon. 3. Combine the steak and banger to form a meaty mixture. 4. Lay out the meat in a rectangle of similar size to the bacon strips. Season with salt and pepper. 5. Roll the meat into a tight roll and refrigerate. 6. Preheat the air fryer to 200ºC. 7. Make a 7×7 bacon weave and roll the bacon weave over the meat, diagonally. 8. Bake for 60 minutes or until the internal temperature reaches at least 74ºC. 9. Let rest for 5 minutes before serving.

Bean and Beef Meatball Taco Pizza

Prep time: 10 minutes | Cook time: 7 to 9 minutes per batch | Serves 4

* 180 g refried beans (from a 450 g can)
* 120 ml salsa
* 10 frozen precooked beef meatballs, thawed and sliced
* 1 jalapeño pepper, sliced
* 4 whole-wheat pitta breads
* 235 g shredded chilli cheese
* 120 g shredded Monterey Jack or Cheddar cheese
* Cooking oil spray
* 80 ml sour cream

1. In a medium bowl, stir together the refried beans, salsa, meatballs, and jalapeño. 2. Insert the crisper plate into the basket and the basket into the unit. Preheat the unit by selecting BAKE, setting the temperature to 190ºC, and setting the time to 3 minutes. Select START/STOP to begin. 3. Top the pittas with the refried bean mixture and sprinkle with the cheeses. 4. Once the unit is preheated, spray the crisper plate with cooking oil. Working in batches, place the pizzas into the basket. Select BAKE, set the temperature to 190ºC, and set the time to 9 minutes. Select START/STOP to begin. 5. After about 7 minutes, check the pizzas. They are done when the cheese is melted and starts to brown. If not ready, resume cooking. 6. When the cooking is complete, top each pizza with a dollop of sour cream and serve warm.

Cantonese BBQ Pork

Prep time: 30 minutes | Cook time: 15 minutes | Serves 4

* 60 ml honey
* 2 tablespoons dark soy sauce
* 1 tablespoon sugar
* 1 tablespoon Shaoxing wine (rice cooking wine)
* 1 tablespoon hoisin sauce
* 2 teaspoons minced garlic
* 2 teaspoons minced fresh ginger
* 1 teaspoon Chinese five-spice powder
* 450 g fatty pork shoulder, cut into long, 1-inch-thick pieces

1. In a small microwave-safe bowl, combine the honey, soy sauce, sugar, wine, hoisin, garlic, ginger, and five-spice powder. Microwave in 10-second intervals, stirring in between, until the honey has dissolved. 2. Use a fork to pierce the pork slices to allow the marinade to penetrate better. Place the pork in a large bowl or resealable plastic bag and pour in half the marinade; set aside the remaining marinade to use for the sauce. Toss to coat. Marinate the pork at room temperature for 30 minutes, or cover and refrigerate for up 24 hours. 3. Place the pork in a single layer in the air fryer basket. Set the air fryer to 200ºC for 15 minutes, turning and basting the pork halfway through the cooking time. 4. While the pork is cooking, microwave the reserved marinade on high for 45 to 60 seconds, stirring every 15 seconds, to thicken it slightly to the consistency of a sauce. 5. Transfer the pork to a cutting board and let rest for 10 minutes. Brush with the sauce and serve.

Mediterranean Beef Steaks

Prep time: 20 minutes | Cook time: 20 minutes | Serves 4

* 2 tablespoons soy sauce or tamari
* 3 heaping tablespoons fresh chives
* 2 tablespoons olive oil
* 3 tablespoons dry white wine
* 4 small-sized beef steaks
* 2 teaspoons smoked cayenne pepper
* ½ teaspoon dried basil
* ½ teaspoon dried rosemary
* 1 teaspoon freshly ground black pepper
* 1 teaspoon sea salt, or more to taste

1. Firstly, coat the steaks with the cayenne pepper, black pepper, salt, basil, and rosemary. 2. Drizzle the steaks with olive oil, white wine, and soy sauce. 3. Finally, roast in the air fryer for 20 minutes at 170ºC. Serve garnished with fresh chives. Bon appétit!

Chapter 6

Poultry

Yakitori

Prep time: 10 minutes | Cook time: 15 minutes | Serves 4

* 120 ml mirin
* 60 ml dry white wine
* 120 ml soy sauce
* 1 tablespoon light brown sugar
* 680 g boneless, skinless chicken thighs, cut into 1½-inch pieces, fat trimmed
* 4 medium spring onions, trimmed, cut into 1½-inch pieces
* Cooking spray
* Special Equipment:
* 4 (4-inch) bamboo skewers, soaked in water for at least 30 minutes

1. Combine the mirin, dry white wine, soy sauce, and brown sugar in a saucepan. Bring to a boil over medium heat. Keep stirring. 2. Boil for another 2 minutes or until it has a thick consistency. Turn off the heat. 3. Preheat the air fryer to 200ºC. Spritz the air fryer basket with cooking spray. 4. Run the bamboo skewers through the chicken pieces and spring onions alternatively. 5. Arrange the skewers in the preheated air fryer, then brush with mirin mixture on both sides. Spritz with cooking spray. 6. Air fry for 10 minutes or until the chicken and spring onions are glossy. Flip the skewers halfway through. 7. Serve immediately.

Chicken Wellington

Prep time: 30 minutes | Cook time: 31 minutes | Serves 2

* 2 (140 g) boneless, skinless chicken breasts
* 120 ml White Worcestershire sauce
* 3 tablespoons butter
* 25 g finely diced onion (about ½ onion)
* 225 g button mushrooms, finely chopped
* 60 ml chicken stock
* 2 tablespoons White
* Worcestershire sauce (or white wine)
* Salt and freshly ground black pepper, to taste
* 1 tablespoon chopped fresh tarragon
* 2 sheets puff pastry, thawed
* 1 egg, beaten
* Vegetable oil

1. Place the chicken breasts in a shallow dish. Pour the White Worcestershire sauce over the chicken coating both sides and marinate for 30 minutes. 2. While the chicken is marinating, melt the butter in a large frying pan over medium-high heat on the stovetop. Add the onion and sauté for a few minutes, until it starts to soften. Add the mushrooms and sauté for 3 to 5 minutes until the vegetables are brown and soft. Deglaze the frying pan with the chicken stock, scraping up any bits from the bottom of the pan. Add the White Worcestershire sauce and simmer for 2 to 3 minutes until the mixture reduces and starts to thicken. Season with salt and freshly ground black pepper. Remove the mushroom mixture from the heat

and stir in the fresh tarragon. Let the mushroom mixture cool. 3. Preheat the air fryer to 180ºC. 4. Remove the chicken from the marinade and transfer it to the air fryer basket. Tuck the small end of the chicken breast under the thicker part to shape it into a circle rather than an oval. Pour the marinade over the chicken and air fry for 10 minutes. 5. Roll out the puff pastry and cut out two 6-inch squares. Brush the perimeter of each square with the egg wash. Place half of the mushroom mixture in the centre of each puff pastry square. Place the chicken breasts, top side down on the mushroom mixture. Starting with one corner of puff pastry and working in one direction, pull the pastry up over the chicken to enclose it and press the ends of the pastry together in the middle. Brush the pastry with the egg wash to seal the edges. Turn the Wellingtons over and set aside. 6. Make a decorative design with the remaining puff pastry, cut out four 10-inch strips. For each Wellington, twist two of the strips together, place them over the chicken breast wrapped in puff pastry, and tuck the ends underneath to seal it. Brush the entire top and sides of the Wellingtons with the egg wash. 7. Preheat the air fryer to 180ºC. . 8. Spray or brush the air fryer basket with vegetable oil. Air fry the chicken Wellingtons for 13 minutes. Carefully turn the Wellingtons over. Air fry for another 8 minutes. Transfer to serving plates, light a candle and enjoy!

Chicken and Gammon Meatballs with Dijon Sauce

Prep time: 10 minutes | Cook time: 15 minutes | Serves 4

* Meatballs:
* 230 g gammon, diced
* 230 g chicken mince
* 110 g grated Swiss cheese
* 1 large egg, beaten
* 3 cloves garlic, minced
* 15 g chopped onions
* 1½ teaspoons sea salt
* 1 teaspoon ground black pepper
* Cooking spray
* Dijon Sauce:
* 3 tablespoons Dijon mustard
* 2 tablespoons lemon juice
* 60 ml chicken broth, warmed
* ¾ teaspoon sea salt
* ¼ teaspoon ground black pepper
* Chopped fresh thyme leaves, for garnish

1. Preheat the air fryer to 200ºC. Spritz the air fryer basket with cooking spray. 2. Combine the ingredients for the meatballs in a large bowl. Stir to mix well, then shape the mixture in twelve 1½-inch meatballs. 3. Arrange the meatballs in a single layer in the air fryer basket. Air fry for 15 minutes or until lightly browned. Flip the balls halfway through. You may need to work in batches to avoid overcrowding. 4. Meanwhile, combine the ingredients, except for the thyme leaves, for the sauce in a small bowl. Stir to mix well. 5. Transfer the cooked meatballs on a large plate, then baste the sauce over. Garnish with thyme leaves and serve.

Blackened Cajun Chicken Tenders

Prep time: 10 minutes | Cook time: 17 minutes | Serves 4

* 2 teaspoons paprika
* 1 teaspoon chilli powder
* ½ teaspoon garlic powder
* ½ teaspoon dried thyme
* ¼ teaspoon onion powder
* ⅛ teaspoon ground
* cayenne pepper
* 2 tablespoons coconut oil
* 450 g boneless, skinless chicken tenders
* 60 ml full-fat ranch dressing

1. In a small bowl, combine all seasonings. 2. Drizzle oil over chicken tenders and then generously coat each tender in the spice mixture. Place tenders into the air fryer basket. 3. Adjust the temperature to (190ºC and air fry for 17 minutes. 4. Tenders will be 76ºC internally when fully cooked. Serve with ranch dressing for dipping.

Crispy Duck with Cherry Sauce

Prep time: 10 minutes | Cook time: 33 minutes | Serves 2 to 4

* 1 whole duck (2.3 kg), split in half, back and rib bones removed
* 1 teaspoon olive oil
* Salt and freshly ground black pepper, to taste
* Cherry Sauce:
* 1 tablespoon butter
* 1 shallot, minced
* 120 ml sherry
* 240 g cherry preserves
* 240 ml chicken stock
* 1 teaspoon white wine vinegar
* 1 teaspoon fresh thyme leaves
* Salt and freshly ground black pepper, to taste

1. Preheat the air fryer to 200ºC. 2. Trim some of the fat from the duck. Rub olive oil on the duck and season with salt and pepper. Place the duck halves in the air fryer basket, breast side up and facing the centre of the basket. 3. Air fry the duck for 20 minutes. Turn the duck over and air fry for another 6 minutes. 4. While duck is air frying, make the cherry sauce. Melt the butter in a large sauté pan. Add the shallot and sauté until it is just starting to brown, about 2 to 3 minutes. Add the sherry and deglaze the pan by scraping up any brown bits from the bottom of the pan. Simmer the liquid for a few minutes, until it has reduced by half. Add the cherry preserves, chicken stock and white wine vinegar. Whisk well to combine all the ingredients. Simmer the sauce until it thickens and coats the back of a spoon, about 5 to 7 minutes. Season with salt and pepper and stir in the fresh thyme leaves. 5. When the air fryer timer goes off, spoon some cherry sauce over the duck and continue to air fry at 200ºC for 4 more minutes. Then, turn the duck halves back over so that the breast side is facing up. Spoon more cherry sauce over the top of the duck, covering the skin completely. Air fry for 3 more minutes and then remove the duck to a plate to rest for a few minutes. 6. Serve the duck in halves, or cut each piece in half again for a smaller serving. Spoon any additional sauce over the duck or serve it on the side.

Chicken Jalfrezi

Prep time: 15 minutes | Cook time: 15 minutes | Serves 4

* Chicken:
* 450 g boneless, skinless chicken thighs, cut into 2 or 3 pieces each
* 1 medium onion, chopped
* 1 large green pepper, stemmed, seeded, and chopped
* 2 tablespoons olive oil
* 1 teaspoon ground turmeric
* 1 teaspoon garam masala
* 1 teaspoon kosher salt
* ½ to 1 teaspoon cayenne pepper
* Sauce:
* 55 g tomato sauce
* 1 tablespoon water
* 1 teaspoon garam masala
* ½ teaspoon kosher salt
* ½ teaspoon cayenne pepper
* Side salad, rice, or naan bread, for serving

1. For the chicken: In a large bowl, combine the chicken, onion, pepper, oil, turmeric, garam masala, salt, and cayenne. Stir and toss until well combined. 2. Place the chicken and vegetables in the air fryer basket. Set the air fryer to 180ºC for 15 minutes, stirring and tossing halfway through the cooking time. Use a meat thermometer to ensure the chicken has reached an internal temperature of 76ºC. 3. Meanwhile, for the sauce: In a small microwave-safe bowl, combine the tomato sauce, water, garam masala, salt, and cayenne. Microwave on high for 1 minute. Remove and stir. Microwave for another minute; set aside. 4. When the chicken is cooked, remove and place chicken and vegetables in a large bowl. Pour the sauce over all. Stir and toss to coat the chicken and vegetables evenly. 5. Serve with rice, naan, or a side salad.

Cornish Hens with Honey-Lime Glaze

Prep time: 15 minutes | Cook time: 25 to 30 minutes | Serves 2 to 3

* 1 small chicken (680 to 900 g)
* 1 tablespoon honey
* 1 tablespoon lime juice
* 1 teaspoon poultry seasoning
* Salt and pepper, to taste
* Cooking spray

1. To split the chicken into halves, cut through breast bone and down one side of the backbone. 2. Mix the honey, lime juice, and poultry seasoning together and brush or rub onto all sides of the chicken. Season to taste with salt and pepper. 3. Spray the air fryer basket with cooking spray and place hen halves in the basket, skin-side down. 4. Air fry at 170ºC for 25 to 30 minutes. Chicken will be done when juices run clear when pierced at leg joint with a fork. Let chicken rest for 5 to 10 minutes before cutting.

Turkey and Cranberry Quesadillas

Prep time: 7 minutes | Cook time: 4 to 8 minutes | Serves 4

* 6 low-sodium whole-wheat tortillas
* 75 g shredded low-sodium low-fat Swiss cheese
* 105 g shredded cooked low-sodium turkey breast
* 2 tablespoons cranberry sauce
* 2 tablespoons dried cranberries
* ½ teaspoon dried basil
* Olive oil spray, for spraying the tortillas

1. Preheat the air fryer to 200°C. 2. Put 3 tortillas on a work surface. 3. Evenly divide the Swiss cheese, turkey, cranberry sauce, and dried cranberries among the tortillas. Sprinkle with the basil and top with the remaining tortillas. 4. Spray the outsides of the tortillas with olive oil spray. 5. One at a time, air fry the quesadillas in the air fryer for 4 to 8 minutes, or until crisp and the cheese is melted. Cut into quarters and serve.

Peanut Butter Chicken Satay

Prep time: 12 minutes | Cook time: 12 to 18 minutes | Serves 4

* 120 g crunchy peanut butter
* 80 ml chicken broth
* 3 tablespoons low-sodium soy sauce
* 2 tablespoons freshly squeezed lemon juice
* 2 garlic cloves, minced
* 2 tablespoons extra-virgin olive oil
* 1 teaspoon curry powder
* 450 g chicken tenders
* Cooking oil spray

1. In a medium bowl, whisk the peanut butter, broth, soy sauce, lemon juice, garlic, olive oil, and curry powder until smooth. 2. Place 2 tablespoons of this mixture into a small bowl. Transfer the remaining sauce to a serving bowl and set aside. 3. Add the chicken tenders to the bowl with the 2 tablespoons of sauce and stir to coat. Let stand for a few minutes to marinate. 4. Insert the crisper plate into the basket and the basket into the unit. Preheat the unit by selecting AIR FRY, setting the temperature to 200°C, and setting the time to 3 minutes. Select START/STOP to begin. 5. Run a 6-inch bamboo skewer lengthwise through each chicken tender. 6. Once the unit is preheated, spray the crisper plate with cooking oil. Working in batches, place half the chicken skewers into the basket in a single layer without overlapping. 7. Select AIR FRY, set the temperature to 200°C, and set the time to 9 minutes. Select START/STOP to begin. 8. After 6 minutes, check the chicken. If a food thermometer inserted into the chicken registers 76°C, it is done. If not, resume cooking. 9. Repeat steps 6, 7, and 8 with the remaining chicken. 10. When the cooking is complete, serve the chicken with the reserved sauce.

Blackened Chicken

Prep time: 10 minutes | Cook time: 20 minutes | Serves 4

* 1 large egg, beaten
* 215 g Blackened seasoning
* 2 whole boneless,
* skinless chicken breasts (about 450 g each), halved
* 1 to 2 tablespoons oil

1. Place the beaten egg in one shallow bowl and the Blackened seasoning in another shallow bowl. 2. One at a time, dip the chicken pieces in the beaten egg and the Blackened seasoning, coating thoroughly. 3. Preheat the air fryer to 180°C. Line the air fryer basket with parchment paper. 4. Place the chicken pieces on the parchment and spritz with oil. 5. Cook for 10 minutes. Flip the chicken, spritz it with oil, and cook for 10 minutes more until the internal temperature reaches 76°C and the chicken is no longer pink inside. Let sit for 5 minutes before serving.

Chicken Paillard

Prep time: 10 minutes | Cook time: 10 minutes | Serves 2

* 2 large eggs, room temperature
* 1 tablespoon water
* 20 g powdered Parmesan cheese or pork dust
* 2 teaspoons dried thyme leaves
* 1 teaspoon ground black pepper
* 2 (140 g) boneless, skinless chicken breasts,
* pounded to ½ inch thick
* Lemon Butter Sauce:
* 2 tablespoons unsalted butter, melted
* 2 teaspoons lemon juice
* ¼ teaspoon finely chopped fresh thyme leaves, plus more for garnish
* ⅛ teaspoon fine sea salt
* Lemon slices, for serving

1. Spray the air fryer basket with avocado oil. Preheat the air fryer to 200°C. 2. Beat the eggs in a shallow dish, then add the water and stir well. 3. In a separate shallow dish, mix together the Parmesan, thyme, and pepper until well combined. 4. One at a time, dip the chicken breasts in the eggs and let any excess drip off, then dredge both sides of the chicken in the Parmesan mixture. As you finish, set the coated chicken in the air fryer basket. 5. Roast the chicken in the air fryer for 5 minutes, then flip the chicken and cook for another 5 minutes, or until cooked through and the internal temperature reaches 76°C. 6. While the chicken cooks, make the lemon butter sauce: In a small bowl, mix together all the sauce ingredients until well combined. 7. Plate the chicken and pour the sauce over it. Garnish with chopped fresh thyme and serve with lemon slices. 8. Store leftovers in an airtight container in the refrigerator for up to 4 days. Reheat in a preheated 200°C air fryer for 5 minutes, or until heated through.

Chapter 6 Poultry 33

Garlic Soy Chicken Thighs

Prep time: 10 minutes | Cook time: 30 minutes | Serves 1 to 2

* 2 tablespoons chicken stock
* 2 tablespoons reduced-sodium soy sauce
* 1½ tablespoons sugar
* 4 garlic cloves, smashed and peeled
* 2 large spring onions, cut into 2- to 3-inch batons, plus more, thinly sliced, for garnish
* 2 bone-in, skin-on chicken thighs (198 to 225 g each)

1. Preheat the air fryer to 190ºC. 2. In a metal cake pan, combine the chicken stock, soy sauce, and sugar and stir until the sugar dissolves. Add the garlic cloves, spring onions, and chicken thighs, turning the thighs to coat them in the marinade, then resting them skin-side up. Place the pan in the air fryer and bake, flipping the thighs every 5 minutes after the first 10 minutes, until the chicken is cooked through and the marinade is reduced to a sticky glaze over the chicken, about 30 minutes. 3. Remove the pan from the air fryer and serve the chicken thighs warm, with any remaining glaze spooned over top and sprinkled with more sliced spring onions.

Air Fried Chicken Potatoes with Sun-Dried Tomato

Prep time: 15 minutes | Cook time: 25 minutes | Serves 2

* 2 teaspoons minced fresh oregano, divided
* 2 teaspoons minced fresh thyme, divided
* 2 teaspoons extra-virgin olive oil, plus extra as needed
* 450 g fingerling potatoes, unpeeled
* 2 (340 g) bone-in split chicken breasts, trimmed
* 1 garlic clove, minced
* 15 g oil-packed sun-dried tomatoes, patted dry and chopped
* 1½ tablespoons red wine vinegar
* 1 tablespoon capers, rinsed and minced
* 1 small shallot, minced
* Salt and ground black pepper, to taste

1. Preheat the air fryer to 180ºC. 2. Combine 1 teaspoon of oregano, 1 teaspoon of thyme, ¼ teaspoon of salt, ¼ teaspoon of ground black pepper, 1 teaspoons of olive oil in a large bowl. Add the potatoes and toss to coat well. 3. Combine the chicken with remaining thyme, oregano, and olive oil. Sprinkle with garlic, salt, and pepper. Toss to coat well. 4. Place the potatoes in the preheated air fryer, then arrange the chicken on top of the potatoes. 5. Air fry for 25 minutes or until the internal temperature of the chicken reaches at least 76ºC and the potatoes are wilted. Flip the chicken and potatoes halfway through. 6. Meanwhile, combine the sun-dried tomatoes, vinegar, capers, and shallot in a separate large bowl. Sprinkle with salt and ground black pepper. Toss

to mix well. 7. Remove the chicken and potatoes from the air fryer and allow to cool for 10 minutes. Serve with the sun-dried tomato mix.

Hawaiian Huli Huli Chicken

Prep time: 30 minutes | Cook time: 15 minutes | Serves 4

* 4 boneless, skinless chicken thighs (680 g)
* 1 (230 g) tin pineapple chunks in juice, drained, 60 ml juice reserved
* 60 ml soy sauce
* 25 g sugar
* 2 tablespoons ketchup
* 1 tablespoon minced fresh ginger
* 1 tablespoon minced garlic
* 25 g chopped spring onions

1. Use a fork to pierce the chicken all over to allow the marinade to penetrate better. Place the chicken in a large bowl or large resealable plastic bag. 2. Set the drained pineapple chunks aside. In a small microwave-safe bowl, combine the pineapple juice, soy sauce, sugar, ketchup, ginger, and garlic. Pour half the sauce over the chicken; toss to coat. Reserve the remaining sauce. Marinate the chicken at room temperature for 30 minutes, or cover and refrigerate for up to 24 hours. 3. Place the chicken in the air fryer basket. (Discard marinade.) Set the air fryer to 180ºC for 15 minutes, turning halfway through the cooking time. 4. Meanwhile, microwave the reserved sauce on high for 45 to 60 seconds, stirring every 15 seconds, until the sauce has the consistency of a thick glaze. 5. At the end of the cooking time, use a meat thermometer to ensure the chicken has reached an internal temperature of 76ºC. 6. Transfer the chicken to a serving platter. Pour the sauce over the chicken. Garnish with the pineapple chunks and spring onions.

Apricot-Glazed Turkey Tenderloin

Prep time: 20 minutes | Cook time: 30 minutes | Serves 4

* Olive oil
* 80 g sugar-free apricot preserves
* ½ tablespoon spicy brown mustard
* 680 g turkey breast tenderloin
* Salt and freshly ground black pepper, to taste

1. Spray the air fryer basket lightly with olive oil. 2. In a small bowl, combine the apricot preserves and mustard to make a paste. 3. Season the turkey with salt and pepper. Spread the apricot paste all over the turkey. 4. Place the turkey in the air fryer basket and lightly spray with olive oil. 5. Air fry at 190ºC for 15 minutes. Flip the turkey over and lightly spray with olive oil. Air fry until the internal temperature reaches at least 80ºC, an additional 10 to 15 minutes. 6. Let the turkey rest for 10 minutes before slicing and serving.

Fajita-Stuffed Chicken Breast

Prep time: 15 minutes | Cook time: 25 minutes | Serves 4

* 2 (170 g) boneless, skinless chicken breasts
* ¼ medium white onion, peeled and sliced
* 1 medium green pepper,
* seeded and sliced
* 1 tablespoon coconut oil
* 2 teaspoons chilli powder
* 1 teaspoon ground cumin
* ½ teaspoon garlic powder

1. Slice each chicken breast completely in half lengthwise into two even pieces. Using a meat tenderizer, pound out the chicken until it's about ¼-inch thickness. 2. Lay each slice of chicken out and place three slices of onion and four slices of green pepper on the end closest to you. Begin rolling the peppers and onions tightly into the chicken. Secure the roll with either toothpicks or a couple pieces of butcher's twine. 3. Drizzle coconut oil over chicken. Sprinkle each side with chilli powder, cumin, and garlic powder. Place each roll into the air fryer basket. 4. Adjust the temperature to 180ºC and air fry for 25 minutes. 5. Serve warm.

Chicken Chimichangas

Prep time: 20 minutes | Cook time: 8 to 10 minutes | Serves 4

* 280 g cooked chicken, shredded
* 2 tablespoons chopped green chilies
* ½ teaspoon oregano
* ½ teaspoon cumin
* ½ teaspoon onion powder
* ¼ teaspoon garlic powder
* Salt and pepper, to taste
* 8 flour tortillas (6- or 7-inch diameter)
* Oil for misting or cooking spray
* Chimichanga Sauce:
* 2 tablespoons butter
* 2 tablespoons flour
* 235 ml chicken broth
* 60 g light sour cream
* ¼ teaspoon salt
* 60 g Pepper Jack or Monterey Jack cheese, shredded

1. Make the sauce by melting butter in a saucepan over medium-low heat. Stir in flour until smooth and slightly bubbly. Gradually add broth, stirring constantly until smooth. Cook and stir 1 minute, until the mixture slightly thickens. Remove from heat and stir in sour cream and salt. Set aside. 2. In a medium bowl, mix together the chicken, chilies, oregano, cumin, onion powder, garlic, salt, and pepper. Stir in 3 to 4 tablespoons of the sauce, using just enough to make the filling moist but not soupy. 3. Divide filling among the 8 corn wraps. Place filling down the centre of maize wrap, stopping about 1 inch from edges. Fold one side of maize wrap over filling, fold the two sides in, and then roll up. Mist all sides with oil or cooking spray. 4. Place chimichangas in air fryer basket seam side down. To fit more into the basket, you tin stand them on their sides with the seams against the sides of the basket. 5. Air fry at 180ºC for 8 to 10 minutes or until heated through and crispy brown outside. 6. Add the shredded cheese to the remaining sauce. Stir over low heat, warming just until the cheese melts. Don't boil or sour cream may curdle. 7. Drizzle the sauce over the chimichangas.

Crisp Paprika Chicken Drumsticks

Prep time: 5 minutes | Cook time: 22 minutes | Serves 2

* 2 teaspoons paprika
* 1 teaspoon packed brown sugar
* 1 teaspoon garlic powder
* ½ teaspoon dry mustard
* ½ teaspoon salt
* Pinch pepper
* 4 (140 g) chicken drumsticks, trimmed
* 1 teaspoon vegetable oil
* 1 scallion, green part only, sliced thin on bias

1. Preheat the air fryer to 200ºC. 2. Combine paprika, sugar, garlic powder, mustard, salt, and pepper in a bowl. Pat drumsticks dry with paper towels. Using metal skewer, poke 10 to 15 holes in skin of each drumstick. Rub with oil and sprinkle evenly with spice mixture. 3. Arrange drumsticks in air fryer basket, spaced evenly apart, alternating ends. Air fry until chicken is crisp and registers 90ºC, 22 to 25 minutes, flipping chicken halfway through cooking. 4. Transfer chicken to serving platter, tent loosely with aluminium foil, and let rest for 5 minutes. Sprinkle with scallion and serve.

Herbed Turkey Breast with Simple Dijon Sauce

Prep time: 5 minutes | Cook time: 30 minutes | Serves 4

* 1 teaspoon chopped fresh sage
* 1 teaspoon chopped fresh tarragon
* 1 teaspoon chopped fresh thyme leaves
* 1 teaspoon chopped fresh rosemary leaves
* 1½ teaspoons sea salt
* 1 teaspoon ground black pepper
* 1 (900 g) turkey breast
* 3 tablespoons Dijon mustard
* 3 tablespoons butter, melted
* Cooking spray

1. Preheat the air fryer to 200ºC. Spritz the air fryer basket with cooking spray. 2. Combine the herbs, salt, and black pepper in a small bowl. Stir to mix well. Set aside. 3. Combine the Dijon mustard and butter in a separate bowl. Stir to mix well. 4. Rub the turkey with the herb mixture on a clean work surface, then brush the turkey with Dijon mixture. 5. Arrange the turkey in the preheated air fryer basket. Air fry for 30 minutes or until an instant-read thermometer inserted in the thickest part of the turkey breast reaches at least 76ºC. 6. Transfer the cooked turkey breast on a large plate and slice to serve.

Cheese-Encrusted Chicken Tenderloins with Peanuts

Prep time: 10 minutes | Cook time: 25 minutes | Serves 4

* 45 g grated Parmesan cheese
* ½ teaspoon garlic powder
* 1 teaspoon red pepper flakes
* Sea salt and ground black pepper, to taste
* 2 tablespoons peanut oil
* 680 g chicken tenderloins
* 2 tablespoons peanuts, roasted and roughly chopped
* Cooking spray

1. Preheat the air fryer to 180ºC. Spritz the air fryer basket with cooking spray. 2. Combine the Parmesan cheese, garlic powder, red pepper flakes, salt, black pepper, and peanut oil in a large bowl. Stir to mix well. 3. Dip the chicken tenderloins in the cheese mixture, then press to coat well. Shake the excess off. 4. Transfer the chicken tenderloins in the air fryer basket. Air fry for 12 minutes or until well browned. Flip the tenderloin halfway through. You may need to work in batches to avoid overcrowding. 5. Transfer the chicken tenderloins on a large plate and top with roasted peanuts before serving.

Italian Chicken with Sauce

Prep time: 15 minutes | Cook time: 20 minutes | Serves 4

* 2 large skinless chicken breasts (about 565 g)
* Salt and freshly ground black pepper
* 25 g ground almonds
* 45 g grated Parmesan cheese
* 2 teaspoons Italian seasoning
* 1 egg, lightly beaten
* 1 tablespoon olive oil
* 225 g no-sugar-added marinara sauce
* 4 slices Mozzarella cheese or 110 g shredded Mozzarella

1. Preheat the air fryer to 180ºC. 2. Slice the chicken breasts in half horizontally to create 4 thinner chicken breasts. Working with one piece at a time, place the chicken between two pieces of parchment paper and pound with a meat mallet or rolling pin to flatten to an even thickness. Season both sides with salt and freshly ground black pepper. 3. In a large shallow bowl, combine the ground almonds, Parmesan, and Italian seasoning; stir until thoroughly combined. Place the egg in another large shallow bowl. 4. Dip the chicken in the egg, followed by the ground almonds mixture, pressing the mixture firmly into the chicken to create an even coating. 5. Working in batches if necessary, arrange the chicken breasts in a single layer in the air fryer basket and coat both sides lightly with olive oil. Pausing halfway through the cooking time to flip the chicken, air fry for 15 minutes, or until a thermometer inserted into the thickest part registers 76ºC. 6. Spoon the marinara sauce over each piece of chicken and top

with the Mozzarella cheese. Air fry for an additional 3 to 5 minutes until the cheese is melted.

Jerk Chicken Thighs

Prep time: 30 minutes | Cook time: 15 to 20 minutes | Serves 6

* 2 teaspoons ground coriander
* 1 teaspoon ground allspice
* 1 teaspoon cayenne pepper
* 1 teaspoon ground ginger
* 1 teaspoon salt
* 1 teaspoon dried thyme
* ½ teaspoon ground cinnamon
* ½ teaspoon ground nutmeg
* 900 g boneless chicken thighs, skin on
* 2 tablespoons olive oil

1. In a small bowl, combine the coriander, allspice, cayenne, ginger, salt, thyme, cinnamon, and nutmeg. Stir until thoroughly combined. 2. Place the chicken in a baking dish and use paper towels to pat dry. Thoroughly coat both sides of the chicken with the spice mixture. Cover and refrigerate for at least 2 hours, preferably overnight. 3. Preheat the air fryer to 180ºC. 4. Working in batches if necessary, arrange the chicken in a single layer in the air fryer basket and lightly coat with the olive oil. Pausing halfway through the cooking time to flip the chicken, air fry for 15 to 20 minutes, until a thermometer inserted into the thickest part registers 76ºC.

Chicken Shawarma

Prep time: 30 minutes | Cook time: 15 minutes | Serves 4

* Shawarma Spice:
* 2 teaspoons dried oregano
* 1 teaspoon ground cinnamon
* 1 teaspoon ground cumin
* 1 teaspoon ground coriander
* 1 teaspoon kosher salt
* ½ teaspoon ground allspice
* ½ teaspoon cayenne
* pepper
* Chicken:
* 450 g boneless, skinless chicken thighs, cut into large bite-size chunks
* 2 tablespoons vegetable oil
* For Serving:
* Tzatziki
* Pita bread

1. For the shawarma spice: In a small bowl, combine the oregano, cayenne, cumin, coriander, salt, cinnamon, and allspice. 2. For the chicken: In a large bowl, toss together the chicken, vegetable oil, and shawarma spice to coat. Marinate at room temperature for 30 minutes or cover and refrigerate for up to 24 hours. 3. Place the chicken in the air fryer basket. Set the air fryer to 180ºC for 15 minutes, or until the chicken reaches an internal temperature of 76ºC. 4. Transfer the chicken to a serving platter. Serve with tzatziki and pita bread.

One-Dish Chicken and Rice

Prep time: 10 minutes | Cook time: 40 minutes | Serves 4

* 190 g long-grain white rice, rinsed and drained
* 120 g cut frozen runner beans (do not thaw)
* 1 tablespoon minced fresh ginger
* 3 cloves garlic, minced
* 1 tablespoon toasted sesame oil
* 1 teaspoon kosher salt
* 1 teaspoon black pepper
* 450 g chicken wings, preferably drumettes

1. In a baking pan, combine the rice, runner beans, ginger, garlic, sesame oil, salt, and pepper. Stir to combine. Place the chicken wings on top of the rice mixture. 2. Cover the pan with foil. Make a long slash in the foil to allow the pan to vent steam. Place the pan in the air fryer basket. Set the air fryer to (190°C for 30 minutes. 3. Remove the foil. Set the air fryer to 200°C for 10 minutes, or until the wings have browned and rendered fat into the rice and vegetables, turning the wings halfway through the cooking time.

Lettuce-Wrapped Turkey and Mushroom Meatballs

Prep time: 10 minutes | Cook time: 15 minutes | Serves 6

* Sauce:
* 2 tablespoons tamari
* 2 tablespoons tomato sauce
* 1 tablespoon lime juice
* ¼ teaspoon peeled and grated fresh ginger
* 1 clove garlic, smashed to a paste
* 120 ml chicken broth
* 55 g sugar
* 2 tablespoons toasted sesame oil
* Cooking spray
* Meatballs:
* 900 g turkey mince
* 75 g finely chopped button mushrooms
* 2 large eggs, beaten
* 1½ teaspoons tamari
* 15 g finely chopped spring onions, plus more for garnish
* 2 teaspoons peeled and grated fresh ginger
* 1 clove garlic, smashed
* 2 teaspoons toasted sesame oil
* 2 tablespoons sugar
* For Serving:
* Lettuce leaves, for serving
* Sliced red chilies, for garnish (optional)
* Toasted sesame seeds, for garnish (optional)

1. Preheat the air fryer to 180°C. Spritz a baking pan with cooking spray. 2. Combine the ingredients for the sauce in a small bowl. Stir to mix well. Set aside. 3. Combine the ingredients for the meatballs in a large bowl. Stir to mix well, then shape the mixture in twelve 1½-inch meatballs. 4. Arrange the meatballs in a single layer on the baking pan, then baste with the sauce. You may need to work in batches to avoid overcrowding. 5. Arrange the pan in the air fryer. Air

fry for 15 minutes or until the meatballs are golden brown. Flip the balls halfway through the cooking time. 6. Unfold the lettuce leaves on a large serving plate, then transfer the cooked meatballs on the leaves. Spread the red chilies and sesame seeds over the balls, then serve.

Apricot-Glazed Chicken Drumsticks

Prep time: 15 minutes | Cook time: 30 minutes | Makes 6 drumsticks

* For the Glaze:
* 160 g apricot preserves
* ½ teaspoon tamari
* ¼ teaspoon chilli powder
* 2 teaspoons Dijon mustard
* For the Chicken:
* 6 chicken drumsticks
* ½ teaspoon seasoning salt
* 1 teaspoon salt
* ½ teaspoon ground black pepper
* Cooking spray

Make the glaze: 1. Combine the ingredients for the glaze in a saucepan, then heat over low heat for 10 minutes or until thickened. 2. Turn off the heat and sit until ready to use. Make the Chicken: 1. Preheat the air fryer to 190°C. Spritz the air fryer basket with cooking spray. 2. Combine the seasoning salt, salt, and pepper in a small bowl. Stir to mix well. 3. Place the chicken drumsticks in the preheated air fryer. Spritz with cooking spray and sprinkle with the salt mixture on both sides. 4. Air fry for 20 minutes or until well browned. Flip the chicken halfway through. 5. Baste the chicken with the glaze and air fryer for 2 more minutes or until the chicken tenderloin is glossy. 6. Serve immediately.

Celery Chicken

Prep time: 10 minutes | Cook time: 15 minutes | Serves 4

* 120 ml soy sauce
* 2 tablespoons hoisin sauce
* 4 teaspoons minced garlic
* 1 teaspoon freshly ground black pepper
* 8 boneless, skinless chicken tenderloins
* 120 g chopped celery
* 1 medium red pepper, diced
* Olive oil spray

1. Preheat the air fryer to 190°C. Spray the air fryer basket lightly with olive oil spray. 2. In a large bowl, mix together the soy sauce, hoisin sauce, garlic, and black pepper to make a marinade. Add the chicken, celery, and pepper and toss to coat. 3. Shake the excess marinade off the chicken, place it and the vegetables in the air fryer basket, and lightly spray with olive oil spray. You may need to cook them in batches. Reserve the remaining marinade. 4. Air fry for 8 minutes. Turn the chicken over and brush with some of the remaining marinade. Air fry for an additional 5 to 7 minutes, or until the chicken reaches an internal temperature of at least 76°C. Serve.

Golden Tenders

Prep time: 10 minutes | Cook time: 15 minutes | Serves 4

* 60 g panko bread crumbs
* 1 tablespoon paprika
* ½ teaspoon salt
* ¼ teaspoon freshly ground black pepper
* 16 chicken tenders
* 115 g mayonnaise
* Olive oil spray

1. In a medium bowl, stir together the panko, paprika, salt, and pepper. 2. In a large bowl, toss together the chicken tenders and mayonnaise to coat. Transfer the coated chicken pieces to the bowl of seasoned panko and dredge to coat thoroughly. Press the coating onto the chicken with your fingers. 3. Insert the crisper plate into the basket and the basket into the unit. Preheat the unit by selecting AIR FRY, setting the temperature to 180ºC, and setting the time to 3 minutes. Select START/STOP to begin. 4. Once the unit is preheated, place a parchment paper liner into the basket. Place the chicken into the basket and spray it with olive oil. 5. Select AIR FRY, set the temperature to 180ºC, and set the time to 15 minutes. Select START/STOP to begin. 6. When the cooking is complete, the tenders will be golden brown and a food thermometer inserted into the chicken should register 76ºC. For more even browning, remove the basket halfway through cooking and flip the tenders. Give them an extra spray of olive oil and reinsert the basket to resume cooking. This ensures they are crispy and brown all over. 7. When the cooking is complete, serve.

Chicken with Bacon and Tomato

Prep time: 25 minutes | Cook time: 10 minutes | Serves 4

* 4 medium-sized skin-on chicken drumsticks
* 1½ teaspoons herbs de Provence
* Salt and pepper, to taste
* 1 tablespoon rice vinegar
* 2 tablespoons olive oil
* 2 garlic cloves, crushed
* 340 g crushed canned tomatoes
* 1 small-size leek, thinly sliced
* 2 slices smoked bacon, chopped

1. Sprinkle the chicken drumsticks with herbs de Provence, salt and pepper; then, drizzle them with rice vinegar and olive oil. 2. Cook in the baking pan at 180ºC for 8 to 10 minutes. Pause the air fryer; stir in the remaining ingredients and continue to cook for 15 minutes longer; make sure to check them periodically. Bon appétit!

Chicken Legs with Leeks

Prep time: 30 minutes | Cook time: 18 minutes | Serves 6

* 2 leeks, sliced
* 2 large-sized tomatoes, chopped
* 3 cloves garlic, minced
* ½ teaspoon dried oregano
* 6 chicken legs, boneless and skinless
* ½ teaspoon smoked cayenne pepper
* 2 tablespoons olive oil
* A freshly ground nutmeg

1. In a mixing dish, thoroughly combine all ingredients, minus the leeks. Place in the refrigerator and let it marinate overnight. 2. Lay the leeks onto the bottom of the air fryer basket. Top with the chicken legs. 3. Roast chicken legs at (190ºC for 18 minutes, turning halfway through. Serve with hoisin sauce.

Chapter 7
Fish and Seafood

Coconut Prawns with Spicy Dipping Sauce

Prep time: 15 minutes | Cook time: 8 minutes | Serves 4

* 70 g pork scratchings
* 70 g desiccated, unsweetened coconut
* 45 g coconut flour
* 1 teaspoon onion powder
* 1 teaspoon garlic powder
* 2 eggs
* 680 g large prawns, peeled and deveined
* ½ teaspoon salt
* ¼ teaspoon freshly ground black pepper
* Spicy Dipping Sauce:
* 115 g mayonnaise
* 2 tablespoons Sriracha
* Zest and juice of ½ lime
* 1 clove garlic, minced

1. Preheat the air fryer to 200ºC. 2. In a food processor fitted with a metal blade, combine the pork scratchings and desiccated coconut. Pulse until the mixture resembles coarse crumbs. Transfer to a shallow bowl. 3. In another shallow bowl, combine the coconut flour, onion powder, and garlic powder; mix until thoroughly combined. 4. In a third shallow bowl, whisk the eggs until slightly frothy. 5. In a large bowl, season the prawns with the salt and pepper, tossing gently to coat. 6. Working a few pieces at a time, dredge the prawns in the flour mixture, followed by the eggs, and finishing with the pork rind crumb mixture. Arrange the prawns on a baking sheet until ready to air fry. 7. Working in batches if necessary, arrange the prawns in a single layer in the air fryer basket. Pausing halfway through the cooking time to turn the prawns, air fry for 8 minutes until cooked through. 8. To make the sauce: In a small bowl, combine the mayonnaise, Sriracha, lime zest and juice, and garlic. Whisk until thoroughly combined. Serve alongside the prawns.

BBQ Prawns with Creole Butter Sauce

Prep time: 10 minutes | Cook time: 12 to 15 minutes | Serves 4

* 6 tablespoons unsalted butter
* 80 ml Worcestershire sauce
* 3 cloves garlic, minced
* Juice of 1 lemon
* 1 teaspoon paprika
* 1 teaspoon Creole seasoning
* 680 g large uncooked prawns, peeled and deveined
* 2 tablespoons fresh parsley

1. Preheat the air fryer to 190ºC. 2. In a large microwave-safe bowl, combine the butter, Worcestershire, and garlic. Microwave on high for 1 to 2 minutes until the butter is melted. Stir in the lemon juice, paprika, and Creole seasoning. Add the prawns and toss until thoroughly coated. 3. Transfer the mixture to a casserole dish or pan that fits in your air fryer. Pausing halfway through the cooking time to turn the prawns, air fry for 12 to 15 minutes, until the prawns are cooked through. Top with the parsley just before serving.

Marinated Swordfish Skewers

Prep time: 30 minutes | Cook time: 6 to 8 minutes | Serves 4

* 455 g filleted swordfish
* 60 ml avocado oil
* 2 tablespoons freshly squeezed lemon juice
* 1 tablespoon minced fresh parsley
* 2 teaspoons Dijon mustard
* Sea salt and freshly ground black pepper, to taste
* 85 g cherry tomatoes

1. Cut the fish into 1½-inch chunks, picking out any remaining bones. 2. In a large bowl, whisk together the oil, lemon juice, parsley, and Dijon mustard. Season to taste with salt and pepper. Add the fish and toss to coat the pieces. Cover and marinate the fish chunks in the refrigerator for 30 minutes. 3. Remove the fish from the marinade. Thread the fish and cherry tomatoes on 4 skewers, alternating as you go. 4. Set the air fryer to 200ºC. Place the skewers in the air fryer basket and air fry for 3 minutes. Flip the skewers and cook for 3 to 5 minutes longer, until the fish is cooked through and an instant-read thermometer reads 60ºC.

Scallops with Asparagus and Peas

Prep time: 10 minutes | Cook time: 7 to 10 minutes | Serves 4

* Cooking oil spray
* 455 g asparagus, ends trimmed, cut into 2-inch pieces
* 100 g sugar snap peas
* 455 g sea scallops
* 1 tablespoon freshly
* squeezed lemon juice
* 2 teaspoons extra-virgin olive oil
* ½ teaspoon dried thyme
* Salt and freshly ground black pepper, to taste

1. Insert the crisper plate into the basket and the basket into the unit. Preheat the unit to 200ºC. 2. Once the unit is preheated, spray the crisper plate with cooking oil. Place the asparagus and sugar snap peas into the basket. 3. Cook for 10 minutes. 4. Meanwhile, check the scallops for a small muscle attached to the side. Pull it off and discard. In a medium bowl, toss together the scallops, lemon juice, olive oil, and thyme. Season with salt and pepper. 5. After 3 minutes, the vegetables should be just starting to get tender. Place the scallops on top of the vegetables. Reinsert the basket to resume cooking. After 3 minutes more, remove the basket and shake it. Again reinsert the basket to resume cooking. 6. When the cooking is complete, the scallops should be firm when tested with your finger and opaque in the center, and the vegetables tender. Serve immediately.

Parmesan Mackerel with Coriander

Prep time: 10 minutes | Cook time: 7 minutes | Serves 2

* 340 g mackerel fillet
* 60 g Parmesan, grated
* 1 teaspoon ground

coriander
* 1 tablespoon olive oil

1. Sprinkle the mackerel fillet with olive oil and put it in the air fryer basket. 2. Top the fish with ground coriander and Parmesan. 3. Cook the fish at 200ºC for 7 minutes.

Prawn Creole Casserole

Prep time: 20 minutes | Cook time: 25 minutes | Serves 4

* 360 g prawns, peeled and deveined
* 50 g chopped celery
* 50 g chopped onion
* 50 g chopped green pepper
* 2 large eggs, beaten
* 240 ml single cream
* 1 tablespoon butter, melted
* 1 tablespoon cornflour
* 1 teaspoon Creole seasoning
* ¾ teaspoon salt
* ½ teaspoon freshly ground black pepper
* 120 g shredded Cheddar cheese
* Cooking spray

1. In a medium bowl, stir together the prawns, celery, onion, and green pepper. 2. In another medium bowl, whisk the eggs, single cream, butter, cornflour, Creole seasoning, salt, and pepper until blended. Stir the egg mixture into the prawn mixture. Add the cheese and stir to combine. 3. Preheat the air fryer to 150ºC. Spritz a baking pan with oil. 4. Transfer the prawn mixture to the prepared pan and place it in the air fryer basket. 5. Bake for 25 minutes, stirring every 10 minutes, until a knife inserted into the center comes out clean. 6. Serve immediately.

Tilapia Almondine

Prep time: 10 minutes | Cook time: 10 minutes | Serves 2

* 25 g almond flour or fine dried bread crumbs
* 2 tablespoons salted butter or ghee, melted
* 1 teaspoon black pepper
* ½ teaspoon kosher or

coarse sea salt
* 60 g mayonnaise
* 2 tilapia fillets
* 435 g thinly sliced almonds
* Vegetable oil spray

1. In a small bowl, mix together the almond flour, butter, pepper and salt. 2. Spread the mayonnaise on both sides of each fish fillet. Dredge the fillets in the almond flour mixture. Spread the sliced almonds on one side of each fillet, pressing lightly to adhere. 3. Spray the air fryer basket with vegetable oil spray. Place the fish fillets in the basket. Set the air fryer to 160ºC for 10 minutes, or until the fish flakes easily with a fork.

Crab Cake Sandwich

Prep time: 15 minutes | Cook time: 10 minutes | Serves 4

* Crab Cakes:
* 60 g panko bread crumbs
* 1 large egg, beaten
* 1 large egg white
* 1 tablespoon mayonnaise
* 1 teaspoon Dijon mustard
* 5 g minced fresh parsley
* 1 tablespoon fresh lemon juice
* ½ teaspoon Old Bay seasoning
* ⅛ teaspoon sweet paprika
* ⅛ teaspoon kosher or coarse sea salt
* Freshly ground black
* pepper, to taste
* 280 g lump crab meat
* Cooking spray
* Cajun Mayo:
* 60 g mayonnaise
* 1 tablespoon minced dill pickle
* 1 teaspoon fresh lemon juice
* ¾ teaspoon Cajun seasoning
* For Serving:
* 4 round lettuce leaves
* 4 whole wheat potato buns or gluten-free buns

1. For the crab cakes: In a large bowl, combine the panko, whole egg, egg white, mayonnaise, mustard, parsley, lemon juice, Old Bay, paprika, salt, and pepper to taste and mix well. Fold in the crab meat, being careful not to over mix. Gently shape into 4 round patties, ¾ inch thick. Spray both sides with oil. 2. Preheat the air fryer to 190ºC. 3. Working in batches, place the crab cakes in the air fryer basket. Air fry for about 10 minutes, flipping halfway, until the edges are golden. 4. Meanwhile, for the Cajun mayo: In a small bowl, combine the mayonnaise, pickle, lemon juice, and Cajun seasoning. 5. To serve: Place a lettuce leaf on each bun bottom and top with a crab cake and a generous tablespoon of Cajun mayonnaise. Add the bun top and serve.

Tuna Cakes

Prep time: 10 minutes | Cook time: 10 minutes | Serves 4

* 4 (85 g) tuna fillets, drained
* 1 large egg, whisked
* 2 tablespoons peeled and

chopped white onion
* ½ teaspoon Old Bay seasoning

1. In a large bowl, mix all ingredients together and form into four patties. 2. Place patties into ungreased air fryer basket. Adjust the temperature to 200ºC and air fry for 10 minutes. Patties will be browned and crispy when done. Let cool 5 minutes before serving.

Chapter 7 Fish and Seafood 41

Baked Monkfish

Prep time: 20 minutes | Cook time: 12 minutes | Serves 2

* 2 teaspoons olive oil
* 100 g celery, sliced
* 2 peppers, sliced
* 1 teaspoon dried thyme
* ½ teaspoon dried marjoram
* ½ teaspoon dried rosemary
* 2 monkfish fillets
* 1 tablespoon coconut aminos, or tamari
* 2 tablespoons lime juice
* Coarse salt and ground black pepper, to taste
* 1 teaspoon cayenne pepper
* 90 g Kalamata olives, pitted and sliced

1. In a nonstick frying pan, heat the olive oil for 1 minute. Once hot, sauté the celery and peppers until tender, about 4 minutes. Sprinkle with thyme, marjoram, and rosemary and set aside. 2. Toss the fish fillets with the coconut aminos, lime juice, salt, black pepper, and cayenne pepper. Place the fish fillets in the lightly greased air fryer basket and bake at 200ºC for 8 minutes. 3. Turn them over, add the olives, and cook an additional 4 minutes. Serve with the sautéed vegetables on the side. Bon appétit!

Air Fried Crab Bun

Prep time: 15 minutes | Cook time: 20 minutes | Serves 2

* 140 g crab meat, chopped
* 2 eggs, beaten
* 2 tablespoons coconut flour
* ¼ teaspoon baking powder
* ½ teaspoon coconut aminos, or tamari
* ½ teaspoon ground black pepper
* 1 tablespoon coconut oil, softened

1. In the mixing bowl, mix crab meat with eggs, coconut flour, baking powder, coconut aminos, ground black pepper, and coconut oil. 2. Knead the smooth dough and cut it into pieces. 3. Make the buns from the crab mixture and put them in the air fryer basket. 4. Cook the crab buns at 190ºC for 20 minutes.

Salmon on Bed of Fennel and Carrot

Prep time: 15 minutes | Cook time: 13 to 14 minutes | Serves 2

* 1 fennel bulb, thinly sliced
* 1 large carrot, peeled and sliced
* 1 small onion, thinly sliced
* 60 ml low-fat sour cream
* ¼ teaspoon coarsely ground pepper
* 2 salmon fillets, 140 g each

1. Combine the fennel, carrot, and onion in a bowl and toss.

2. Put the vegetable mixture into a baking pan. Roast in the air fryer at200ºC for 4 minutes or until the vegetables are crisp-tender. 3. Remove the pan from the air fryer. Stir in the sour cream and sprinkle the vegetables with the pepper. 4. Top with the salmon fillets. 5. Return the pan to the air fryer. Roast for another 9 to 10 minutes or until the salmon just barely flakes when tested with a fork.

Asian Swordfish

Prep time: 10 minutes | Cook time: 6 to 11 minutes | Serves 4

* 4 swordfish steaks, 100 g each
* ½ teaspoon toasted sesame oil
* 1 red chilli, finely minced
* 2 garlic cloves, grated
* 1 tablespoon grated fresh
* ginger
* ½ teaspoon Chinese five-spice powder
* ⅛ teaspoon freshly ground black pepper
* 2 tablespoons freshly squeezed lemon juice

1. Place the swordfish steaks on a work surface and drizzle with the sesame oil. 2. In a small bowl, mix the jalapeño, garlic, ginger, five-spice powder, pepper, and lemon juice. Rub this mixture into the fish and let it stand for 10 minutes. 3. Roast the swordfish in the air fryer at 190ºC for 6 to 11 minutes, or until the swordfish reaches an internal temperature of at least 60ºC on a meat thermometer. Serve immediately.

Prawns Curry

Prep time: 30 minutes | Cook time: 10 minutes | Serves 4

* 180 ml unsweetened full-fat coconut milk
* 10 g finely chopped brown onion
* 2 teaspoons garam masala
* 1 tablespoon minced fresh ginger
* 1 tablespoon minced garlic
* 1 teaspoon ground
* turmeric
* 1 teaspoon salt
* ¼ to ½ teaspoon cayenne pepper
* 455 g raw prawns (21 to 25 count), peeled and deveined
* 2 teaspoons chopped fresh coriander

1. In a large bowl, stir together the coconut milk, onion, garam masala, ginger, garlic, turmeric, salt and cayenne, until well blended. 2. Add the prawns and toss until coated with sauce on all sides. Marinate at room temperature for 30 minutes. 3. Transfer the prawns and marinade to a baking pan. Place the pan in the air fryer basket. Set the air fryer to 190ºC for 10 minutes, stirring halfway through the cooking time. 4. Transfer the prawns to a serving bowl or platter. Sprinkle with the coriander and serve.

Apple Cider Mussels

Prep time: 10 minutes | Cook time: 2 minutes | Serves 5

* 900 g mussels, cleaned and de-bearded
* 1 teaspoon onion powder
* 1 teaspoon ground cumin
* 1 tablespoon avocado oil
* 60 ml apple cider vinegar

1. Mix mussels with onion powder, ground cumin, avocado oil, and apple cider vinegar. 2. Put the mussels in the air fryer and cook at 200°C for 2 minutes.

Jalea

Prep time: 20 minutes | Cook time: 10 minutes | Serves 4

* Salsa Criolla:
* ½ red onion, thinly sliced
* 2 tomatoes, diced
* 1 serrano or red chilli, deseeded and diced
* 1 clove garlic, minced
* 5 g chopped fresh coriander
* Pinch of kosher or coarse sea salt
* 3 limes
* Fried Seafood:
* 455 g firm, white-fleshed fish such as cod (add an extra 230 g fish if not using prawns)
* 20 large or jumbo prawns, peeled and deveined
* 20 g plain flour
* 20 g cornflour
* 1 teaspoon garlic powder
* 1 teaspoon kosher or coarse sea salt
* ¼ teaspoon cayenne pepper
* 120 g panko bread crumbs
* 2 eggs, beaten with 2 tablespoons water
* Vegetable oil, for spraying
* Mayonnaise or tartar sauce, for serving (optional)

1. To make the Salsa Criolla, combine the red onion, tomatoes, pepper, garlic, coriander, and salt in a medium bowl. Add the juice and zest of 2 of the limes. Refrigerate the salad while you make the fish. 2. To make the seafood, cut the fish fillets into strips approximately 2 inches long and 1 inch wide. Place the flour, cornflour, garlic powder, salt, and cayenne pepper on a plate and whisk to combine. Place the panko on a separate plate. Dredge the fish strips in the seasoned flour mixture, shaking off any excess. Dip the strips in the egg mixture, coating them completely, then dredge in the panko, shaking off any excess. Place the fish strips on a plate or rack. Repeat with the prawns, if using. 3. Spray the air fryer basket with oil, and preheat the air fryer to 200°C. Working in 2 or 3 batches, arrange the fish and prawns in a single layer in the basket, taking care not to crowd the basket. Spray with oil. Air fry for 5 minutes, then flip and air fry for another 4 to 5 minutes until the outside is brown and crisp and the inside of the fish is opaque and flakes easily with a fork. Repeat with the remaining seafood. 4. Place the fried seafood on a platter. Use a slotted spoon to remove the salsa criolla from the bowl, leaving behind any liquid that has accumulated. Place the salsa criolla on top of the fried seafood. Serve immediately with the remaining lime, cut into wedges, and mayonnaise or tartar sauce as desired.

Catfish Bites

Prep time: 15 minutes | Cook time: 20 minutes | Serves 4

* Olive or vegetable oil, for spraying
* 455 g catfish fillets, cut into 2-inch pieces
* 235 ml buttermilk
* 35 g cornmeal
* 20 g plain flour
* 2 teaspoons Creole seasoning
* 120 ml yellow mustard

1. Line the air fryer basket with baking paper and spray lightly with oil. 2. Place the catfish pieces and buttermilk in a zip-top plastic bag, seal, and refrigerate for about 10 minutes. 3. In a shallow bowl, mix together the cornmeal, flour, and Creole seasoning. 4. Remove the catfish from the bag and pat dry with a paper towel. 5. Spread the mustard on all sides of the catfish, then dip them in the cornmeal mixture until evenly coated. 6. Place the catfish in the prepared basket. You may need to work in batches, depending on the size of your air fryer. Spray lightly with oil. 7. Air fry at 200°C for 10 minutes, flip carefully, spray with oil, and cook for another 10 minutes. Serve immediately.

Oyster Po'Boy

Prep time: 20 minutes | Cook time: 5 minutes | Serves 4

* 55 g plain flour
* 20 g yellow cornmeal
* 1 tablespoon Cajun seasoning
* 1 teaspoon salt
* 2 large eggs, beaten
* 1 teaspoon hot sauce
* 455 g pre-shucked oysters
* 1 (12-inch) French
* baguette, quartered and sliced horizontally
* Tartar Sauce, as needed
* 150 g shredded lettuce, divided
* 2 tomatoes, cut into slices
* Cooking spray

1. In a shallow bowl, whisk the flour, cornmeal, Cajun seasoning, and salt until blended. In a second shallow bowl, whisk together the eggs and hot sauce. 2. One at a time, dip the oysters in the cornmeal mixture, the eggs, and again in the cornmeal, coating thoroughly. 3. Preheat the air fryer to 200°C. Line the air fryer basket with baking paper. 4. Place the oysters on the baking paper and spritz with oil. 5. Air fry for 2 minutes. Shake the basket, spritz the oysters with oil, and air fry for 3 minutes more until lightly browned and crispy. 6. Spread each sandwich half with Tartar Sauce. Assemble the po'boys by layering each sandwich with fried oysters, ½ cup shredded lettuce, and 2 tomato slices. 7. Serve immediately.

Chapter 7 Fish and Seafood 43

Scallops in Lemon-Butter Sauce

Prep time: 10 minutes | Cook time: 6 minutes | Serves 2

* 8 large dry sea scallops (about 340 g)
* Salt and freshly ground black pepper, to taste
* 2 tablespoons olive oil
* 2 tablespoons unsalted butter, melted
* 2 tablespoons chopped
* flat-leaf parsley
* 1 tablespoon fresh lemon juice
* 2 teaspoons capers, drained and chopped
* 1 teaspoon grated lemon zest
* 1 clove garlic, minced

1. Preheat the air fryer to 200°C. 2. Use a paper towel to pat the scallops dry. Sprinkle lightly with salt and pepper. Brush with the olive oil. Arrange the scallops in a single layer in the air fryer basket. Pausing halfway through the cooking time to turn the scallops, air fry for about 6 minutes until firm and opaque. 3. Meanwhile, in a small bowl, combine the oil, butter, parsley, lemon juice, capers, lemon zest, and garlic. Drizzle over the scallops just before serving.

Crunchy Air Fried Cod Fillets

Prep time: 10 minutes | Cook time: 12 minutes | Serves 2

* 20 g panko bread crumbs
* 1 teaspoon vegetable oil
* 1 small shallot, minced
* 1 small garlic clove, minced
* ½ teaspoon minced fresh thyme
* Salt and pepper, to taste
* 1 tablespoon minced
* fresh parsley
* 1 tablespoon mayonnaise
* 1 large egg yolk
* ¼ teaspoon grated lemon zest, plus lemon wedges for serving
* 2 (230 g) skinless cod fillets, 1¼ inches thick
* Vegetable oil spray

1. Preheat the air fryer to 150°C. 2. Make foil sling for air fryer basket by folding 1 long sheet of aluminium foil so it is 4 inches wide. Lay sheet of foil widthwise across basket, pressing foil into and up sides of basket. Fold excess foil as needed so that edges of foil are flush with top of basket. Lightly spray the foil and basket with vegetable oil spray. 3. Toss the panko with the oil in a bowl until evenly coated. Stir in the shallot, garlic, thyme, ¼ teaspoon salt, and ⅛ teaspoon pepper. Microwave, stirring frequently, until the panko is light golden brown, about 2 minutes. Transfer to a shallow dish and let cool slightly; stir in the parsley. Whisk the mayonnaise, egg yolk, lemon zest, and ⅛ teaspoon pepper together in another bowl. 4. Pat the cod dry with paper towels and season with salt and pepper. Arrange the fillets, skinned-side down, on plate and brush tops evenly with mayonnaise mixture. (Tuck thinner tail ends of fillets under themselves as needed to create uniform pieces.) Working with 1 fillet at a time, dredge the coated side in panko mixture, pressing

gently to adhere. Arrange the fillets, crumb-side up, on sling in the prepared basket, spaced evenly apart. 5. Bake for 12 to 16 minutes, using a sling to rotate fillets halfway through cooking. Using a sling, carefully remove cod from air fryer. Serve with the lemon wedges.

Garlic Butter Prawns Scampi

Prep time: 5 minutes | Cook time: 8 minutes | Serves 4

* Sauce:
* 60 g unsalted butter
* 2 tablespoons fish stock or chicken broth
* 2 cloves garlic, minced
* 2 tablespoons chopped fresh basil leaves
* 1 tablespoon lemon juice
* 1 tablespoon chopped fresh parsley, plus more
* for garnish
* 1 teaspoon red pepper flakes
* Prawns:
* 455 g large prawns, peeled and deveined, tails removed
* Fresh basil sprigs, for garnish

1. Preheat the air fryer to 180°C. 2. Put all the ingredients for the sauce in a baking pan and stir to incorporate. 3. Transfer the baking pan to the air fryer and air fry for 3 minutes, or until the sauce is heated through. 4. Once done, add the prawns to the baking pan, flipping to coat in the sauce. 5. Return to the air fryer and cook for another 5 minutes, or until the prawns are pink and opaque. Stir the prawns twice during cooking. 6. Serve garnished with the parsley and basil sprigs.

Fish Gratin

Prep time: 30 minutes | Cook time: 17 minutes | Serves 4

* 1 tablespoon avocado oil
* 455 g hake fillets
* 1 teaspoon garlic powder
* Sea salt and ground white pepper, to taste
* 2 tablespoons shallots, chopped
* 1 pepper, seeded and chopped
* 110 g cottage cheese
* 120 ml sour cream
* 1 egg, well whisked
* 1 teaspoon yellow mustard
* 1 tablespoon lime juice
* 60 g Swiss cheese, shredded

1. Brush the bottom and sides of a casserole dish with avocado oil. Add the hake fillets to the casserole dish and sprinkle with garlic powder, salt, and pepper. 2. Add the chopped shallots and peppers. 3. In a mixing bowl, thoroughly combine the Cottage cheese, sour cream, egg, mustard, and lime juice. Pour the mixture over fish and spread evenly. 4. Cook in the preheated air fryer at 190°C for 10 minutes. 5. Top with the Swiss cheese and cook an additional 7 minutes. Let it rest for 10 minutes before slicing and serving. Bon appétit!

Friday Night Fish-Fry

Prep time: 10 minutes | Cook time: 10 minutes | Serves 4

* 1 large egg
* 25 g powdered Parmesan cheese
* 1 teaspoon smoked paprika
* ¼ teaspoon celery salt
* ¼ teaspoon ground black
* pepper
* 4 cod fillets, 110 g each
* Chopped fresh oregano or parsley, for garnish (optional)
* Lemon slices, for serving (optional)

1. Spray the air fryer basket with avocado oil. Preheat the air fryer to 200°C. 2. Crack the egg in a shallow bowl and beat it lightly with a fork. Combine the Parmesan cheese, paprika, celery salt, and pepper in a separate shallow bowl. 3. One at a time, dip the fillets into the egg, then dredge them in the Parmesan mixture. Using your hands, press the Parmesan onto the fillets to form a nice crust. As you finish, place the fish in the air fryer basket. 4. Air fry the fish in the air fryer for 10 minutes, or until it is cooked through and flakes easily with a fork. Garnish with fresh oregano or parsley and serve with lemon slices, if desired. 5. Store leftovers in an airtight container in the refrigerator for up to 3 days. Reheat in a preheated 200°C air fryer for 5 minutes, or until warmed through.

Panko Catfish Nuggets

Prep time: 10 minutes | Cook time: 7 to 8 minutes | Serves 4

* 2 medium catfish fillets, cut into chunks (approximately 1 × 2 inch)
* Salt and pepper, to taste
* 2 eggs
* 2 tablespoons skimmed milk
* 30 g cornflour
* 75 g panko bread crumbs
* Cooking spray

1. Preheat the air fryer to 200°C. 2. In a medium bowl, season the fish chunks with salt and pepper to taste. 3. In a small bowl, beat together the eggs with milk until well combined. 4. Place the cornflour and bread crumbs into separate shallow dishes. 5. Dredge the fish chunks one at a time in the cornflour, coating well on both sides, then dip in the egg mixture, shaking off any excess, finally press well into the bread crumbs. Spritz the fish chunks with cooking spray. 6. Arrange the fish chunks in the air fryer basket in a single layer. You may need to cook in batches depending on the size of your air fryer basket. 7. Fry the fish chunks for 7 to 8 minutes until they are no longer translucent in the center and golden brown. Shake the basket once during cooking. 8. Remove the fish chunks from the basket to a plate. Repeat with the remaining fish chunks. 9. Serve warm.

Paprika Prawns

Prep time: 5 minutes | Cook time: 6 minutes | Serves 2

* 230 g medium prawns, peeled and deveined
* 2 tablespoons salted butter, melted
* 1 teaspoon paprika
* ½ teaspoon garlic powder
* ¼ teaspoon onion powder
* ½ teaspoon Old Bay seasoning

1. Toss all ingredients together in a large bowl. Place prawns into the air fryer basket. 2. Adjust the temperature to 200°C and set the timer for 6 minutes. 3. Turn the prawns halfway through the cooking time to ensure even cooking. Serve immediately.

Air Fryer Fish Fry

Prep time: 5 minutes | Cook time: 15 minutes | Serves 4

* 470 ml low-fat buttermilk
* ½ teaspoon garlic powder
* ½ teaspoon onion powder
* 4 (110 g) sole fillets
* 35 g plain yellow cornmeal
* 25 g chickpea flour
* ¼ teaspoon cayenne pepper
* Freshly ground black pepper

1. In a large bowl, combine the buttermilk, garlic powder, and onion powder. 2. Add the sole, turning until well coated, and set aside to marinate for 20 minutes. 3. In a shallow bowl, stir the cornmeal, chickpea flour, cayenne, and pepper together. 4. Dredge the fillets in the meal mixture, turning until well coated. Place in the basket of an air fryer. 5. Set the air fryer to 190°C, close, and cook for 12 minutes.

Blackened Red Snapper

Prep time: 13 minutes | Cook time: 8 to 10 minutes | Serves 4

* 1½ teaspoons black pepper
* ¼ teaspoon thyme
* ¼ teaspoon garlic powder
* ⅛ teaspoon cayenne pepper
* 1 teaspoon olive oil
* 4 red snapper fillet portions, skin on, 110 g each
* 4 thin slices lemon
* Cooking spray

1. Mix the spices and oil together to make a paste. Rub into both sides of the fish. 2. Spray the air fryer basket with nonstick cooking spray and lay snapper steaks in basket, skin-side down. 3. Place a lemon slice on each piece of fish. 4. Roast at 200°C for 8 to 10 minutes. The fish will not flake when done, but it should be white through the center.

Chilli Tilapia

Prep time: 5 minutes | Cook time: 20 minutes | Serves 4

* 4 tilapia fillets, boneless
* 1 teaspoon chilli flakes
* 1 teaspoon dried oregano
* 1 tablespoon avocado oil
* 1 teaspoon mustard

1. Rub the tilapia fillets with chilli flakes, dried oregano, avocado oil, and mustard and put in the air fryer. 2. Cook it for 10 minutes per side at 180°C.

Coriander Lime Baked Salmon

Prep time: 10 minutes | Cook time: 12 minutes | Serves 2

* 2 salmon fillets, 85 g each, skin removed
* 1 tablespoon salted butter, melted
* 1 teaspoon chilli powder
* ½ teaspoon finely minced garlic
* 20 g sliced pickled jalapeños
* ½ medium lime, juiced
* 2 tablespoons chopped coriander

1. Place salmon fillets into a round baking pan. Brush each with butter and sprinkle with chilli powder and garlic. 2. Place jalapeño slices on top and around salmon. Pour half of the lime juice over the salmon and cover with foil. Place pan into the air fryer basket. 3. Adjust the temperature to 190°C and bake for 12 minutes. 4. When fully cooked, salmon should flake easily with a fork and reach an internal temperature of at least 64°C. 5. To serve, spritz with remaining lime juice and garnish with coriander.

Breaded Prawns Tacos

Prep time: 10 minutes | Cook time: 9 minutes | Makes 8 tacos

* 2 large eggs
* 1 teaspoon prepared yellow mustard
* 455 g small prawns, peeled, deveined, and tails removed
* 45 g finely shredded Gouda or Parmesan cheese
* 80 g pork scratchings ground to dust
* For Serving:
* 8 large round lettuce leaves
* 60 ml pico de gallo
* 20 g shredded purple cabbage
* 1 lemon, sliced
* Guacamole (optional)

1. Preheat the air fryer to 200°C. 2. Crack the eggs into a large bowl, add the mustard, and whisk until well combined. Add the prawns and stir well to coat. 3. In a medium-sized bowl, mix together the cheese and pork scratching dust until well combined. 4. One at a time, roll the coated prawns in the pork scratching dust mixture and use your hands to press it onto each prawns. Spray the coated prawns with avocado oil and place them in the air fryer basket, leaving space between them. 5. Air fry the prawns for 9 minutes, or until cooked through and no longer translucent, flipping after 4 minutes. 6. To serve, place a lettuce leaf on a serving plate, place several prawns on top, and top with 1½ teaspoons each of pico de gallo and purple cabbage. Squeeze some lemon juice on top and serve with guacamole, if desired. 7. Store leftover prawns in an airtight container in the refrigerator for up to 3 days. Reheat in a preheated 200°C air fryer for 5 minutes, or until warmed through.

Chapter 8
Vegetables and Sides

Parsnip Fries with Romesco Sauce

Prep time: 20 minutes | Cook time: 24 minutes | Serves 4

* Romesco Sauce:
* 1 red pepper, halved and seeded
* 1 (1-inch) thick slice of Italian bread, torn into pieces
* 130 g almonds, toasted
* Olive oil
* ½ Red chilli, seeded
* 1 tablespoon fresh parsley leaves
* 1 clove garlic
* 2 plum tomatoes, peeled
* and seeded
* 1 tablespoon red wine vinegar
* ¼ teaspoon smoked paprika
* ½ teaspoon salt
* 180 ml olive oil
* 3 parsnips, peeled and cut into long strips
* 2 teaspoons olive oil
* Salt and freshly ground black pepper, to taste

1. Preheat the air fryer to 200ºC. 2. Place the red pepper halves, cut side down, in the air fryer basket and air fry for 8 to 10 minutes, or until the skin turns black all over. Remove the pepper from the air fryer and let it cool. When it is cool enough to handle, peel the pepper. 3. Toss the torn bread and almonds with a little olive oil and air fry for 4 minutes, shaking the basket a couple times throughout the cooking time. When the bread and almonds are nicely toasted, remove them from the air fryer and let them cool for just a minute or two. 4. Combine the toasted bread, almonds, roasted red pepper, Red chilli, parsley, garlic, tomatoes, vinegar, smoked paprika and salt in a food processor or blender. Process until smooth. With the processor running, add the olive oil through the feed tube until the sauce comes together in a smooth paste that is barely pourable. 5. Toss the parsnip strips with the olive oil, salt and freshly ground black pepper and air fry at 200ºC for 10 minutes, shaking the basket a couple times during the cooking process so they brown and cook evenly. Serve the parsnip fries warm with the Romesco sauce to dip into.

Citrus Sweet Potatoes and Carrots

Prep time: 5 minutes | Cook time: 20 to 25 minutes | Serves 4

* 2 large carrots, cut into 1-inch chunks
* 1 medium sweet potato, peeled and cut into 1-inch cubes
* 25 g chopped onion
* 2 garlic cloves, minced
* 2 tablespoons honey
* 1 tablespoon freshly squeezed orange juice
* 2 teaspoons butter, melted

1. Insert the crisper plate into the basket and the basket into the unit. Preheat the unit by selecting AIR ROAST, setting the temperature to 200ºC, and setting the time to 3 minutes. Select START/STOP to begin. 2. In a 6-by-2-inch round pan, toss together the carrots, sweet potato, onion, garlic, honey, orange juice, and melted butter to coat. 3. Once the unit is preheated, place the pan into the basket. 4. Select AIR ROAST, set the temperature to 200ºC, and set the time to 25 minutes. Select START/STOP to begin. 5. After 15 minutes, remove the basket and shake the vegetables. Reinsert the basket to resume cooking. After 5 minutes, if the vegetables are tender and glazed, they are done. If not, resume cooking. 6. When the cooking is complete, serve immediately.

Easy Potato Croquettes

Prep time: 15 minutes | Cook time: 15 minutes | Serves 10

* 55 g nutritional yeast
* 300 g boiled potatoes, mashed
* 1 flax egg
* 1 tablespoon flour
* 2 tablespoons chopped
* chives
* Salt and ground black pepper, to taste
* 2 tablespoons vegetable oil
* 30 g bread crumbs

1. Preheat the air fryer to 200ºC. 2. In a bowl, combine the nutritional yeast, potatoes, flax egg, flour, and chives. Sprinkle with salt and pepper as desired. 3. In a separate bowl, mix the vegetable oil and bread crumbs to achieve a crumbly consistency. 4. Shape the potato mixture into small balls and dip each one into the bread crumb mixture. 5. Put the croquettes inside the air fryer and air fry for 15 minutes, ensuring the croquettes turn golden brown. 6. Serve immediately.

Sesame Carrots and Sugar Snap Peas

Prep time: 10 minutes | Cook time: 16 minutes | Serves 4

* 450 g carrots, peeled sliced on the bias (½-inch slices)
* 1 teaspoon olive oil
* Salt and freshly ground black pepper, to taste
* 110 g honey
* 1 tablespoon sesame oil
* 1 tablespoon soy sauce
* ½ teaspoon minced fresh ginger
* 110 g sugar snap peas
* 1½ teaspoons sesame seeds

1. Preheat the air fryer to 180ºC. 2. Toss the carrots with the olive oil, season with salt and pepper and air fry for 10 minutes, shaking the basket once or twice during the cooking process. 3. Combine the honey, sesame oil, soy sauce and minced ginger in a large bowl. Add the sugar snap peas and the air-fried carrots to the honey mixture, toss to coat and return everything to the air fryer basket. 4. Turn up the temperature to 200ºC and air fry for an additional 6 minutes, shaking the basket once during the cooking process. 5. Transfer the carrots and sugar snap peas to a serving bowl. Pour the sauce from the bottom of the cooker over the vegetables and sprinkle sesame seeds over top. Serve immediately.

Tingly Chili-Roasted Broccoli

Prep time: 5 minutes | Cook time: 10 minutes | Serves 2

* 340 g broccoli florets
* 2 tablespoons Asian hot chilli oil
* 1 teaspoon ground Sichuan peppercorns (or black pepper)
* 2 garlic cloves, finely chopped
* 1 (2-inch) piece fresh ginger, peeled and finely chopped
* coarse sea salt and freshly ground black pepper, to taste

1. In a bowl, toss together the broccoli, chilli oil, Sichuan peppercorns, garlic, ginger, and salt and black pepper to taste. 2. Transfer to the air fryer and roast at 190°C, shaking the basket halfway through, until lightly charred and tender, about 10 minutes. Remove from the air fryer and serve warm.

Garlic Courgette and Red Peppers

Prep time: 5 minutes | Cook time: 15 minutes | Serves 6

* 2 medium courgette, cubed
* 1 red pepper, diced
* 2 garlic cloves, sliced
* 2 tablespoons olive oil
* ½ teaspoon salt

1. Preheat the air fryer to 193°C. 2. In a large bowl, mix together the courgette, pepper, and garlic with the olive oil and salt. 3. Pour the mixture into the air fryer basket, and roast for 7 minutes. Shake or stir, then roast for 7 to 8 minutes more.

Easy Greek Briami (Ratatouille)

Prep time: 15 minutes | Cook time: 40 minutes | Serves 6

* 2 Maris Piper potatoes, cubed
* 100 g plum tomatoes, cubed
* 1 aubergine, cubed
* 1 courgette, cubed
* 1 red onion, chopped
* 1 red pepper, chopped
* 2 garlic cloves, minced
* 1 teaspoon dried mint
* 1 teaspoon dried parsley
* 1 teaspoon dried oregano
* ½ teaspoon salt
* ½ teaspoon black pepper
* ¼ teaspoon red pepper flakes
* 80 ml olive oil
* 1 (230 g) tin tomato paste
* 65 ml vegetable stock
* 65 ml water

1. Preheat the air fryer to 160°C. 2. In a large bowl, combine the potatoes, tomatoes, aubergine, courgette onion, pepper, garlic, mint, parsley, oregano, salt, black pepper, and red pepper flakes. 3. In a small bowl, mix together the olive oil, tomato paste, stock, and water. 4. Pour the oil-and-tomato-paste mixture over the vegetables and toss until everything is coated. 5. Pour the coated vegetables into the air fryer basket in an even layer and roast for 20 minutes. After 20 minutes, stir well and spread out again. Roast for an additional 10 minutes, then repeat the process and cook for another 10 minutes.

Parmesan Herb Focaccia Bread

Prep time: 10 minutes | Cook time: 10 minutes | Serves 6

* 225 g shredded Mozzarella cheese
* 30 g full-fat cream cheese
* 95 g blanched finely ground almond flour
* 40 g ground golden flaxseed
* 20 g grated Parmesan cheese
* ½ teaspoon bicarbonate of soda
* 2 large eggs
* ½ teaspoon garlic powder
* ¼ teaspoon dried basil
* ¼ teaspoon dried rosemary
* 2 tablespoons salted butter, melted and divided

1. Place Mozzarella, cream cheese, and almond flour into a large microwave-safe bowl and microwave for 1 minute. Add the flaxseed, Parmesan, and bicarbonate of soda and stir until smooth ball forms. If the mixture cools too much, it will be hard to mix. Return to microwave for 10 to 15 seconds to rewarm if necessary. 2. Stir in eggs. You may need to use your hands to get them fully incorporated. Just keep stirring and they will absorb into the dough. 3. Sprinkle dough with garlic powder, basil, and rosemary and knead into dough. Grease a baking pan with 1 tablespoon melted butter. Press the dough evenly into the pan. Place pan into the air fryer basket. 4. Adjust the temperature to 200°C and bake for 10 minutes. 5. At 7 minutes, cover with foil if bread begins to get too dark. 6. Remove and let cool at least 30 minutes. Drizzle with remaining butter and serve.

Glazed Carrots

Prep time: 10 minutes | Cook time: 8 to 10 minutes | Serves 4

* 2 teaspoons honey
* 1 teaspoon orange juice
* ½ teaspoon grated orange rind
* ⅛ teaspoon ginger
* 450 g baby carrots
* 2 teaspoons olive oil
* ¼ teaspoon salt

1. Combine honey, orange juice, grated rind, and ginger in a small bowl and set aside. 2. Toss the carrots, oil, and salt together to coat well and pour them into the air fryer basket. 3. Roast at 200°C for 5 minutes. Shake basket to stir a little and cook for 2 to 4 minutes more, until carrots are barely tender. 4. Pour carrots into a baking pan. 5. Stir the honey mixture to combine well, pour glaze over carrots, and stir to coat. 6. Roast at 180°C for 1 minute or just until heated through.

Chapter 8 Vegetables and Sides 49

Roasted Brussels Sprouts with Orange and Garlic

Prep time: 5 minutes | Cook time: 10 minutes | Serves 4

* 450 g Brussels sprouts, quartered
* 2 garlic cloves, minced
* 2 tablespoons olive oil
* ½ teaspoon salt
* 1 orange, cut into rings

1. Preheat the air fryer to 180ºC. 2. In a large bowl, toss the quartered Brussels sprouts with the garlic, olive oil, and salt until well coated. 3. Pour the Brussels sprouts into the air fryer, lay the orange slices on top of them, and roast for 10 minutes. 4. Remove from the air fryer and set the orange slices aside. Toss the Brussels sprouts before serving.

Rosemary-Roasted Red Potatoes

Prep time: 5 minutes | Cook time: 20 minutes | Serves 6

* 450 g red potatoes, quartered
* 65 ml olive oil
* ½ teaspoon coarse sea
* salt
* ¼ teaspoon black pepper
* 1 garlic clove, minced
* 4 rosemary sprigs

1. Preheat the air fryer to 180ºC. 2. In a large bowl, toss the potatoes with the olive oil, salt, pepper, and garlic until well coated. 3. Pour the potatoes into the air fryer basket and top with the sprigs of rosemary. 4. Roast for 10 minutes, then stir or toss the potatoes and roast for 10 minutes more. 5. Remove the rosemary sprigs and serve the potatoes. Season with additional salt and pepper, if needed.

Broccoli with Sesame Dressing

Prep time: 5 minutes | Cook time: 10 minutes | Serves 4

* 425 g broccoli florets, cut into bite-size pieces
* 1 tablespoon olive oil
* ¼ teaspoon salt
* 2 tablespoons sesame seeds
* 2 tablespoons rice vinegar
* 2 tablespoons coconut aminos
* 2 tablespoons sesame oil
* ½ teaspoon xylitol
* ¼ teaspoon red pepper flakes (optional)

1. Preheat the air fryer to 200ºC. 2. In a large bowl, toss the broccoli with the olive oil and salt until thoroughly coated. 3. Transfer the broccoli to the air fryer basket. Pausing halfway through the cooking time to shake the basket, air fry for 10 minutes until the stems are tender and the edges are beginning to crisp. 4. Meanwhile, in the same large bowl, whisk together the sesame seeds, vinegar, coconut aminos, sesame oil, xylitol, and red pepper flakes (if using). 5. Transfer the broccoli to the bowl and toss until thoroughly coated with the seasonings. Serve warm or at room temperature.

Maize and Coriander Salad

Prep time: 10 minutes | Cook time: 10 minutes | Serves 2

* 2 ears of maize, shucked (halved crosswise if too large to fit in your air fryer)
* 1 tablespoon unsalted butter, at room temperature
* 1 teaspoon chilli powder
* ¼ teaspoon garlic powder
* coarse sea salt and freshly ground black pepper, to
* taste
* 20 g lightly packed fresh coriander leaves
* 1 tablespoon sour cream
* 1 tablespoon mayonnaise
* 1 teaspoon adobo sauce (from a tin of chipotle peppers in adobo sauce)
* 2 tablespoons crumbled feta cheese
* Lime wedges, for serving

1. Brush the maize all over with the butter, then sprinkle with the chilli powder and garlic powder, and season with salt and pepper. Place the maize in the air fryer and air fry at 200ºC, turning over halfway through, until the kernels are lightly charred and tender, about 10 minutes. 2. Transfer the ears to a cutting board, let stand 1 minute, then carefully cut the kernels off the cobs and move them to a bowl. Add the coriander leaves and toss to combine (the coriander leaves will wilt slightly). 3. In a small bowl, stir together the sour cream, mayonnaise, and adobo sauce. Divide the maize and coriander among plates and spoon the adobo dressing over the top. Sprinkle with the feta cheese and serve with lime wedges on the side.

Butternut Marrow Croquettes

Prep time: 5 minutes | Cook time: 17 minutes | Serves 4

* ⅓ butternut marrow, peeled and grated
* 40 g plain flour
* 2 eggs, whisked
* 4 cloves garlic, minced
* 1½ tablespoons olive oil
* 1 teaspoon fine sea salt
* ⅓ teaspoon freshly ground black pepper, or more to taste
* ⅓ teaspoon dried sage
* A pinch of ground allspice

1. Preheat the air fryer to 170ºC. Line the air fryer basket with parchment paper. 2. In a mixing bowl, stir together all the ingredients until well combined. 3. Make the marrow croquettes: Use a small biscuit scoop to drop tablespoonfuls of the marrow mixture onto a lightly floured surface and shape into balls with your hands. Transfer them to the air fryer basket. 4. Air fry for 17 minutes until the marrow croquettes are golden brown. 5. Remove from the basket to a plate and serve warm.

Cauliflower with Lime Juice

Prep time: 10 minutes | Cook time: 7 minutes | Serves 4

* 215 g chopped cauliflower florets
* 2 tablespoons coconut oil, melted
* 2 teaspoons chilli powder
* ½ teaspoon garlic powder
* 1 medium lime
* 2 tablespoons chopped coriander

1. In a large bowl, toss cauliflower with coconut oil. Sprinkle with chilli powder and garlic powder. Place seasoned cauliflower into the air fryer basket. 2. Adjust the temperature to 180°C and set the timer for 7 minutes. 3. Cauliflower will be tender and begin to turn golden at the edges. Place into a serving bowl. 4. Cut the lime into quarters and squeeze juice over cauliflower. Garnish with coriander.

Chiles Rellenos with Red Chile Sauce

Prep time: 20 minutes | Cook time: 20 minutes | Serves 2

* Peppers:
* 2 poblano peppers, rinsed and dried
* 110 g thawed frozen or drained canned maize kernels
* 1 spring onion, sliced
* 2 tablespoons chopped fresh coriander
* ½ teaspoon coarse sea salt
* ¼ teaspoon black pepper
* 150 g grated Monterey Jack cheese
* Sauce:
* 3 tablespoons extra-virgin
* olive oil
* 25 g finely chopped brown onion
* 2 teaspoons minced garlic
* 1 (170 g) tin tomato paste
* 2 tablespoons ancho chilli powder
* 1 teaspoon dried oregano
* 1 teaspoon ground cumin
* ½ teaspoon coarse sea salt
* 470 ml chicken stock
* 2 tablespoons fresh lemon juice
* Mexican crema or sour cream, for serving

1. For the peppers: Place the peppers in the air fryer basket. Set the air fryer to 200°C for 10 minutes, turning the peppers halfway through the cooking time, until their skins are charred. Transfer the peppers to a resealable plastic bag, seal, and set aside to steam for 5 minutes. Peel the peppers and discard the skins. Cut a slit down the centre of each pepper, starting at the stem and continuing to the tip. Remove the seeds, being careful not to tear the chilli. 2. In a medium bowl, combine the maize, spring onion, coriander, salt, black pepper, and cheese; set aside. 3. Meanwhile, for the sauce: In a large frying pan, heat the olive oil over medium-high heat. Add the onion and cook, stirring, until tender, about 5 minutes. Add the garlic and cook, stirring, for 30 seconds. Stir in the tomato paste, chilli powder, oregano, and cumin, and salt. Cook, stirring, for 1 minute. Whisk in the stock and lemon juice. Bring to a simmer and cook, stirring occasionally, while the stuffed peppers finish cooking. 4. Cut a slit down the centre of each poblano pepper, starting at the stem and continuing to the tip. Remove the seeds, being careful not to tear the chilli. 5. Carefully stuff each pepper with half the maize mixture. Place the stuffed peppers in a baking pan. Place the pan in the air fryer basket. Set the air fryer to 200°C for 10 minutes, or until the cheese has melted. 6. Transfer the stuffed peppers to a serving platter and drizzle with the sauce and some crema.

Southwestern Roasted Maize

Prep time: 10 minutes | Cook time: 10 minutes | Serves 4

* maize:
* 240 g thawed frozen maize kernels
* 50 g diced brown onion
* 150 g mixed diced peppers
* 1 jalapeño, diced
* 1 tablespoon fresh lemon juice
* 1 teaspoon ground cumin
* ½ teaspoon ancho chilli
* powder
* ½ teaspoon coarse sea salt
* For Serving:
* 150 g queso fresco or feta cheese
* 10 g chopped fresh coriander
* 1 tablespoon fresh lemon juice

1. For the maize: In a large bowl, stir together the maize, onion, peppers, jalapeño, lemon juice, cumin, chilli powder, and salt until well incorporated. 2. Pour the spiced vegetables into the air fryer basket. Set the air fryer to 190°C for 10 minutes, stirring halfway through the cooking time. 3. Transfer the maize mixture to a serving bowl. Add the cheese, coriander, and lemon juice and stir well to combine. Serve immediately.

Parmesan-Thyme Butternut Marrow

Prep time: 15 minutes | Cook time: 20 minutes | Serves 4

* 350 g butternut marrow, cubed into 1-inch pieces (approximately 1 medium)
* 2 tablespoons olive oil
* ¼ teaspoon salt
* ¼ teaspoon garlic powder
* ¼ teaspoon black pepper
* 1 tablespoon fresh thyme
* 20 g grated Parmesan

1. Preheat the air fryer to 180°C. 2. In a large bowl, combine the cubed marrow with the olive oil, salt, garlic powder, pepper, and thyme until the marrow is well coated. 3. Pour this mixture into the air fryer basket, and roast for 10 minutes. Stir and roast another 8 to 10 minutes more. 4. Remove the marrow from the air fryer and toss with freshly grated Parmesan before serving.

Courgette Balls

Prep time: 5 minutes | Cook time: 10 minutes | Serves 4

* 4 courgettes
* 1 egg
* 45 g grated Parmesan
* cheese
* 1 tablespoon Italian herbs
* 75 g grated coconut

1. Thinly grate the courgettes and dry with a cheesecloth, ensuring to remove all the moisture. 2. In a bowl, combine the courgettes with the egg, Parmesan, Italian herbs, and grated coconut, mixing well to incorporate everything. Using the hands, mould the mixture into balls. 3. Preheat the air fryer to 200ºC. 4. Lay the courgette balls in the air fryer basket and air fry for 10 minutes. 5. Serve hot.

Crispy Garlic Sliced Aubergine

Prep time: 5 minutes | Cook time: 25 minutes | Serves 4

* 1 egg
* 1 tablespoon water
* 60 g whole wheat bread crumbs
* 1 teaspoon garlic powder
* ½ teaspoon dried oregano
* ½ teaspoon salt
* ½ teaspoon paprika
* 1 medium aubergine, sliced into ¼-inch-thick rounds
* 1 tablespoon olive oil

1. Preheat the air fryer to 180ºC. 2. In a medium shallow bowl, beat together the egg and water until frothy. 3. In a separate medium shallow bowl, mix together bread crumbs, garlic powder, oregano, salt, and paprika. 4. Dip each aubergine slice into the egg mixture, then into the bread crumb mixture, coating the outside with crumbs. Place the slices in a single layer in the bottom of the air fryer basket. 5. Drizzle the tops of the aubergine slices with the olive oil, then fry for 15 minutes. Turn each slice and cook for an additional 10 minutes.

Bread Rolls

Prep time: 10 minutes | Cook time: 12 minutes | Serves 6

* 225 g shredded Mozzarella cheese
* 30 g full-fat cream cheese
* 95 g blanched finely ground almond flour
* 40 g ground flaxseed
* ½ teaspoon baking powder
* 1 large egg

1. Place Mozzarella, cream cheese, and almond flour in a large microwave-safe bowl. Microwave for 1 minute. Mix until smooth. 2. Add flaxseed, baking powder, and egg until fully combined and smooth. Microwave an additional 15 seconds if it becomes too firm. 3. Separate the dough into six pieces and roll into balls. Place the balls into the air fryer basket. 4. Adjust the temperature to 160ºC and air fry for 12 minutes. 5. Allow rolls to cool completely before serving.

Broccoli-Cheddar Twice-Baked Potatoes

Prep time: 10 minutes | Cook time: 46 minutes | Serves 4

* Oil, for spraying
* 2 medium Maris Piper potatoes
* 1 tablespoon olive oil
* 30 g broccoli florets
* 1 tablespoon sour cream
* 1 teaspoon garlic powder
* 1 teaspoon onion powder
* 60 g shredded Cheddar cheese

1. Line the air fryer basket with parchment and spray lightly with oil. 2. Rinse the potatoes and pat dry with paper towels. Rub the outside of the potatoes with the olive oil and place them in the prepared basket. 3. Air fry at 200ºC for 40 minutes, or until easily pierced with a fork. Let cool just enough to handle, then cut the potatoes in half lengthwise. 4. Meanwhile, place the broccoli in a microwave-safe bowl, cover with water, and microwave on high for 5 to 8 minutes. Drain and set aside. 5. Scoop out most of the potato flesh and transfer to a medium bowl. 6. Add the sour cream, garlic, and onion powder and stir until the potatoes are mashed. 7. Spoon the potato mixture back into the hollowed potato skins, mounding it to fit, if necessary. Top with the broccoli and cheese. Return the potatoes to the basket. You may need to work in batches, depending on the size of your air fryer. 8. Air fry at 200ºC for 3 to 6 minutes, or until the cheese has melted. Serve immediately.

Indian Aubergine Bharta

Prep time: 15 minutes | Cook time: 20 minutes | Serves 4

* 1 medium aubergine
* 2 tablespoons vegetable oil
* 25 g finely minced onion
* 100 g finely chopped fresh tomato
* 2 tablespoons fresh lemon
* juice
* 2 tablespoons chopped fresh coriander
* ½ teaspoon coarse sea salt
* ⅛ teaspoon cayenne pepper

1. Rub the aubergine all over with the vegetable oil. Place the aubergine in the air fryer basket. Set the air fryer to 200ºC for 20 minutes, or until the aubergine skin is blistered and charred. 2. Transfer the aubergine to a re-sealable plastic bag, seal, and set aside for 15 to 20 minutes (the aubergine will finish cooking in the residual heat trapped in the bag). 3. Transfer the aubergine to a large bowl. Peel off and discard the charred skin. Roughly mash the aubergine flesh. Add the onion, tomato, lemon juice, coriander, salt, and cayenne. Stir to combine.

Asparagus Fries

Prep time: 15 minutes | Cook time: 5 to 7 minutes per batch | Serves 4

* 340 g fresh asparagus spears with tough ends trimmed off
* 2 egg whites
* 60 ml water
* 80 g panko bread crumbs
* 25 g grated Parmesan cheese, plus 2 tablespoons
* ¼ teaspoon salt
* Oil for misting or cooking spray

1. Preheat the air fryer to 200°C. 2. In a shallow dish, beat egg whites and water until slightly foamy. 3. In another shallow dish, combine panko, Parmesan, and salt. 4. Dip asparagus spears in egg, then roll in crumbs. Spray with oil or cooking spray. 5. Place a layer of asparagus in air fryer basket, leaving just a little space in between each spear. Stack another layer on top, crosswise. Air fry at 200°C for 5 to 7 minutes, until crispy and golden brown. 6. Repeat to cook remaining asparagus.

Chapter 9
Vegetarian Mains

Savoury Gigantes Plaki (Baked Giant White Beans)

Prep time: 5 minutes | Cook time: 30 minutes | Serves 4

* Olive oil cooking spray
* 1 (425 g) can cooked butter beans, drained and rinsed
* 235 ml diced fresh tomatoes
* ½ tablespoon tomato paste
* 2 garlic cloves, minced
* ½ brown onion, diced
* ½ teaspoon salt
* 60 ml olive oil
* 60 ml fresh parsley, chopped

1. Preheat the air fryer to 192°C. 2. Lightly coat the inside of a 1.2 L capacity casserole dish with olive oil cooking spray. (The shape of the casserole dish will depend upon the size of the air fryer, but it needs to be able to hold at least 1.2 L.) 3. In a large bowl, combine the butter beans, tomatoes, tomato paste, garlic, onion, salt, and olive oil, mixing until all ingredients are combined. 4. Pour the mixture into the prepared casserole dish and top with the chopped parsley. 5. Bake in the air fryer for 15 minutes. 6. Stir well, then return to the air fryer and bake for 15 minutes more.

Sweet Potato Black Bean Burgers

Prep time: 10 minutes | Cook time: 10 minutes | Serves 4

* 1 (425 g) can black beans, drained and rinsed
* 235 ml mashed sweet potato
* ½ teaspoon dried oregano
* ¼ teaspoon dried thyme
* ¼ teaspoon dried marjoram
* 1 garlic clove, minced
* ¼ teaspoon salt
* ¼ teaspoon black pepper
* 1 tablespoon lemon juice
* 235 ml cooked brown rice
* 60 to 120 ml wholemeal breadcrumbs
* 1 tablespoon olive oil
* For serving:
* Wholemeal buns or wholemeal pittas
* Plain Greek yoghurt
* Avocado
* Lettuce
* Tomato
* Red onion

1. Preheat the air fryer to 192°C. 2. In a large bowl, use the back of a fork to mash the black beans until there are no large pieces left. 3. Add the mashed sweet potato, oregano, thyme, marjoram, garlic, salt, pepper, and lemon juice, and mix until well combined. 4. Stir in the cooked rice. 5. Add in 60 ml wholemeal breadcrumbs and stir. 6. Check to see if the mixture is dry enough to form patties. If it seems too wet and loose, add an additional 60 ml breadcrumbs and stir. 7. Form the dough into 4 patties. 8. Place them into the air fryer basket in a single layer, making sure that they don't touch each other. 9. Brush half of the olive oil onto the patties and bake for 5 minutes. 10. Flip the patties over, brush the other side with the remaining oil and bake for an additional 4 to 5 minutes. 11. Serve on toasted wholemeal buns or wholemeal pittas with a spoonful of yoghurt and avocado, lettuce, tomato, and red onion as desired.

Rosemary Beetroots with Balsamic Glaze

Prep time: 5 minutes | Cook time: 10 minutes | Serves 2

* Beetroot:
* 2 beetroots, cubed
* 2 tablespoons olive oil
* 2 sprigs rosemary, chopped
* Salt and black pepper, to taste
* Balsamic Glaze:
* 80 ml balsamic vinegar
* 1 tablespoon honey

1. Preheat the air fryer to 200°C. 2.Combine the beetroots, olive oil, rosemary, salt, and pepper in a mixing bowl and toss until the beetroots are completely coated. 3.Place the beetroots in the air fryer basket and air fry for 10 minutes until the beetroots are crisp and browned at the edges. 4.Shake the basket halfway through the cooking time. 5.Meanwhile, make the balsamic glaze: Place the balsamic vinegar and honey in a small saucepan and bring to a boil over medium heat. 6.When the sauce starts to boil, reduce the heat to medium-low heat and simmer until the liquid is reduced by half. 7.When ready, remove the beetroots from the basket to a platter. 8.Pour the balsamic glaze over the top and serve immediately.

Baked Courgette

Prep time: 10 minutes | Cook time: 8 minutes | Serves 4

* 2 tablespoons salted butter
* 60 g diced white onion
* ½ teaspoon minced garlic
* 120 ml double cream
* 60 g full fat soft white cheese
* 235 g shredded extra mature Cheddar cheese
* 2 medium courgette, spiralized

1. In a large saucepan over medium heat, melt butter. 2.Add onion and sauté until it begins to soften, 1 to 3 minutes. 3.Add garlic and sauté for 30 seconds, then pour in cream and add soft white cheese. 4.Remove the pan from heat and stir in Cheddar. 5.Add the courgette and toss in the sauce, then put into a round baking dish. 6.Cover the dish with foil and place into the air fryer basket. 7.Adjust the temperature to 190°C and set the timer for 8 minutes. 8.After 6 minutes remove the foil and let the top brown for remaining cooking time. 9.Stir and serve.

Gold Ravioli

Prep time: 10 minutes | Cook time: 6 minutes | Serves 4

* 120 g panko breadcrumbs
* 2 teaspoons Engevita yeast flakes
* 1 teaspoon dried basil
* 1 teaspoon dried oregano
* 1 teaspoon garlic powder
* Salt and ground black pepper, to taste
* 60 g aquafaba or egg alternative
* 227 g ravioli
* Cooking spray

1. Cover the air fryer basket with aluminium foil and coat with a light brushing of oil. 2.Preheat the air fryer to 200°C. 3.Combine the panko breadcrumbs, Engevita yeast flakes, basil, oregano, and garlic powder. 4.Sprinkle with salt and pepper to taste. 5.Put the aquafaba in a separate bowl. 6.Dip the ravioli in the aquafaba before coating it in the panko mixture. 7.Spritz with cooking spray and transfer to the air fryer. 8.Air fry for 6 minutes. 9.Shake the air fryer basket halfway. 10.Serve hot.

Broccoli Crust Pizza

Prep time: 15 minutes | Cook time: 12 minutes | Serves 4

* 700 g riced broccoli, steamed and drained well
* 1 large egg
* 120 g grated vegetarian Parmesan cheese
* 3 tablespoons low-carb Alfredo sauce
* 120 g shredded Mozzarella cheese

1. In a large bowl, mix broccoli, egg, and Parmesan. 2.Cut a piece of parchment to fit your air fryer basket. 3.Press out the pizza mixture to fit on the parchment, working in two batches if necessary. 4.Place into the air fryer basket. 5.Adjust the temperature to 190°C and air fry for 5 minutes. 6.The crust should be firm enough to flip. 7.If not, add 2 additional minutes. 8.Flip crust. 9.Top with Alfredo sauce and Mozzarella. 10.Return to the air fryer basket and cook an additional 7 minutes or until cheese is golden and bubbling. 11.Serve warm.

Crispy Fried Okra with Chilli

Prep time: 5 minutes | Cook time: 10 minutes | Serves 4

* 3 tablespoons sour cream
* 2 tablespoons flour
* 2 tablespoons semolina
* ½ teaspoon red chilli powder
* Salt and black pepper, to taste
* 450 g okra, halved
* Cooking spray

1. Preheat the air fryer to 200°C. 2.Spray the air fryer basket with cooking spray. 3.In a shallow bowl, place the sour cream. 4.In another shallow bowl, thoroughly combine the flour, semolina, red chilli powder, salt, and pepper. 5.Dredge the okra in the sour cream, then roll in the flour mixture until evenly coated. 6.Arrange the okra in the air fryer basket and air fry for 10 minutes, flipping the okra halfway through, or until golden brown and crispy. 7.Cool for 5 minutes before serving.

Crispy Cabbage Steaks

Prep time: 5 minutes | Cook time: 10 minutes | Serves 4

* 1 small head green cabbage, cored and cut into ½-inch-thick slices
* ¼ teaspoon salt
* ¼ teaspoon ground black pepper
* 2 tablespoons olive oil
* 1 clove garlic, peeled and finely minced
* ½ teaspoon dried thyme
* ½ teaspoon dried parsley

1. Sprinkle each side of cabbage with salt and pepper, then place into ungreased air fryer basket, working in batches if needed. 2.Drizzle each side of cabbage with olive oil, then sprinkle with remaining ingredients on both sides. 3.Adjust the temperature to 180°C and air fry for 10 minutes, turning "steaks" halfway through cooking. 4.3.Cabbage will be browned at the edges and tender when done. 5.Serve warm.

Fried Root Vegetable Medley with Thyme

Prep time: 10 minutes | Cook time: 22 minutes | Serves 4

* 2 carrots, sliced
* 2 potatoes, cut into chunks
* 1 swede, cut into chunks
* 1 turnip, cut into chunks
* 1 beetroot, cut into chunks
* 8 shallots, halved
* 2 tablespoons olive oil
* Salt and black pepper, to taste
* 2 tablespoons tomato pesto
* 2 tablespoons water
* 2 tablespoons chopped fresh thyme

1. Preheat the air fryer to 200°C. 2.Toss the carrots, potatoes, swede, turnip, beetroot, shallots, olive oil, salt, and pepper in a large mixing bowl until the root vegetables are evenly coated. 3.Place the root vegetables in the air fryer basket and air fry for 12 minutes. 4.Shake the basket and air fry for another 10 minutes until they are cooked to your preferred doneness. 5.Meanwhile, in a small bowl, whisk together the tomato pesto and water until smooth. 6.When ready, remove the root vegetables from the basket to a platter. 7.Drizzle with the tomato pesto mixture and sprinkle with the thyme. 8.Serve immediately.

Quiche-Stuffed Peppers

Prep time: 5 minutes | Cook time: 15 minutes | Serves 2

* 2 medium green peppers
* 3 large eggs
* 60 g full-fat ricotta cheese
* 60 g diced brown onion
* 120 g chopped broccoli
* 120 g shredded medium Cheddar cheese

1. Cut the tops off of the peppers and remove the seeds and white membranes with a small knife. 2.In a medium bowl, whisk eggs and ricotta. 3.Add onion and broccoli. 4.Pour the egg and vegetable mixture evenly into each pepper. 5.Top with Cheddar. 6.Place peppers into a 1 L round baking dish and place into the air fryer basket. 7.Adjust the temperature to 180ºC and bake for 15 minutes. 8.Eggs will be mostly firm and peppers tender when fully cooked. 9.Serve immediately.

Chapter 10

Desserts

Cinnamon Rolls with Cream Glaze

Prep time: 2 hours 15 minutes | Cook time: 10 minutes | Serves 8

* 450 g frozen bread dough, thawed
* 2 tablespoons melted butter
* 1½ tablespoons cinnamon
* 100 g brown sugar
* Cooking spray
* Cream Glaze:
* 110 g soft white cheese
* ½ teaspoon vanilla extract
* 2 tablespoons melted butter
* 150 g powdered erythritol

1. Place the bread dough on a clean work surface, then roll the dough out into a rectangle with a rolling pin 2.Brush the top of the dough with melted butter and leave 1-inch edges uncovered 3.Combine the cinnamon and sugar in a small bowl, then sprinkle the dough with the cinnamon mixture 4.Roll the dough over tightly, then cut the dough log into 8 portions 5.Wrap the portions in plastic, better separately, and let sit to rise for 1 or 2 hours 6.Meanwhile, combine the ingredients for the glaze in a separate small bowl 7.Stir to mix well 8.Preheat the air fryer to 180ºC 9.Spritz the air fryer basket with cooking spray 10.Transfer the risen rolls to the preheated air fryer 11.You may need to work in batches to avoid overcrowding 12.Air fry for 5 minutes or until golden brown 13.Flip the rolls halfway through 14.Serve the rolls with the glaze.

Strawberry Scone Shortcake

Prep time: 10 minutes | Cook time: 20 minutes | Serves 4 to 6

* 90 g Plain flour
* 3 tablespoons granulated sugar
* 1½ teaspoons baking powder
* 1 teaspoon kosher, or coarse sea salt
* 8 tablespoons unsalted butter, cubed and chilled
* 315 ml double cream, chilled
* Turbinado (raw cane) sugar, for sprinkling
* 2 tablespoons icing sugar, plus more for dusting
* ½ teaspoon vanilla extract
* 165 g quartered fresh strawberries

1. In a large bowl, whisk together the flour, granulated sugar, baking powder, and salt. Add the butter and use your fingers to break apart the butter pieces while working them into the flour mixture, until pea-size pieces form. Pour 155 mlof the cream over the flour mixture and, using a rubber spatula, mix the ingredients together until just combined. 2. Transfer the dough to a work surface and form into a 7-inch-wide disk. Brush the top with water, then sprinkle with some turbinado sugar. Using a large metal spatula, transfer the dough to the air fryer and bake at 180ºC until golden brown and fluffy, about 20 minutes. Let cool in the air fryer basket for 5 minutes, then turn out onto a wire rack, right-side up, to cool completely. 3.

Meanwhile, in a bowl, beat the remaining 155 ml of cream, the icing sugar, and vanilla until stiff peaks form. Split the scone like a hamburger bun and spread the strawberries over the bottom. Top with the whipped cream and cover with the top of the scone. Dust with icing sugar and cut into wedges to serve.

Sweet Potato Donut Holes

Prep time: 10 minutes | Cook time: 4 to 5 minutes per batch | Makes 18 donut holes

* 65 g Plain flour
* 50 g granulated sugar
* ¼ teaspoon baking soda
* 1 teaspoon baking powder
* ⅛ teaspoon salt
* 125 g cooked & mashed purple sweet potatoes
* 1 egg, beaten
* 2 tablespoons butter, melted
* 1 teaspoon pure vanilla extract
* Coconut, or avocado oil for misting or cooking spray

1. Preheat the air fryer to 200ºC. 2. In a large bowl, stir together the flour, sugar, baking soda, baking powder, and salt. 3. In a separate bowl, combine the potatoes, egg, butter, and vanilla and mix well. 4. Add potato mixture to dry ingredients and stir into a soft dough. 5. Shape dough into 1½-inch balls. Mist lightly with oil or cooking spray. 6. Place 9 donut holes in air fryer basket, leaving a little space in between. Cook for 4 to 5 minutes, until done in center and lightly browned outside. 7. Repeat step 6 to cook remaining donut holes.

5-Ingredient Brownies

Prep time: 10 minutes | Cook time: 25 minutes | Serves 6

* Vegetable oil
* 110 g unsalted butter
* ½ cup chocolate crisps
* 3 large eggs
* 80 g granulated sugar
* 1 teaspoon pure vanilla extract

1. Generously grease a baking pan with vegetable oil. 2. In a microwave-safe bowl, combine the butter and chocolate crisps. Microwave on high for 1 minute. Stir very well. (You want the heat from the butter and chocolate to melt the remaining clumps. If you microwave until everything melts, the chocolate will be overcooked. If necessary, microwave for an additional 10 seconds, but stir well before you try that.) 3. In a medium bowl, combine the eggs, sugar, and vanilla. Whisk until light and frothy. Whisking continuously, slowly pour in the melted chocolate in a thin stream and whisk until everything is incorporated. 4. Pour the batter into the prepared pan. Set the pan in the air fryer basket. Set the air fryer to 180ºC, and bake for 25 minutes, or until a toothpick inserted into the center comes out clean. 5. Let cool in the pan on a wire rack for 30 minutes before cutting into squares.

Indian Toast and Milk

Prep time: 10 minutes | Cook time: 20 minutes | Serves 4

* 305 g sweetened, condensed milk
* 240 ml evaporated milk
* 240 ml single cream
* 1 teaspoon ground cardamom, plus additional for garnish
* 1 pinch saffron threads
* 4 slices white bread
* 2 to 3 tablespoons ghee or butter, softened
* 2 tablespoons crushed pistachios, for garnish (optional)

1. In a baking pan, combine the condensed milk, evaporated milk, half-and-half, cardamom, and saffron. Stir until well combined. 2. Place the pan in the air fryer basket. Set the air fryer to 180°C for 15 minutes, stirring halfway through the cooking time. Remove the sweetened milk from the air fryer and set aside. 3. Cut each slice of bread into two triangles. Brush each side with ghee. Place the bread in the air fryer basket. Keeping the air fryer on 180°C cook for 5 minutes or until golden brown and toasty. 4. Remove the bread from the air fryer. Arrange two triangles in each of four wide, shallow bowls. Pour the hot milk mixture on top of the bread and let soak for 30 minutes. 5. Garnish with pistachios if using, and sprinkle with additional cardamom.

Peach Fried Pies

Prep time: 15 minutes | Cook time: 20 minutes | Makes 8 pies

* 420 g tin sliced peaches in heavy syrup
* 1 teaspoon ground cinnamon
* 1 tablespoon cornflour
* 1 large egg
* All-purpose flour, for dusting
* Half a sheet of shortcrust pastry cut into 2

1. Reserving 2 tablespoons of syrup, drain the peaches well. Chop the peaches into bite-size pieces, transfer to a medium bowl, and stir in the cinnamon. 2. In a small bowl, stir together the reserved peach juice and cornflour until dissolved. Stir this slurry into the peaches. 3. In another small bowl, beat the egg. 4. Dust a cutting board or work surface with flour and spread the piecrusts on the prepared surface. Using a knife, cut each crust into 4 squares (8 squares total). 5. Place 2 tablespoons of peaches onto each dough square. Fold the dough in half and seal the edges. Using a pastry brush, spread the beaten egg on both sides of each hand pie. Using a knife, make 2 thin slits in the top of each pie. 6. Preheat the air fryer to 180°C. 7. Line the air fryer basket with baking paper. Place 4 pies on the baking paper. 8. Cook for 10 minutes. Flip the pies, brush with beaten egg, and cook for 5 minutes more. Repeat with the remaining pies.

Fried Oreos

Prep time: 7 minutes | Cook time: 6 minutes per batch | Makes 12 cookies

* Coconut, or avocado oil for misting, or nonstick spray
* 120 g ready-made pancake mix
* 1 teaspoon vanilla extract
* 120 ml water, plus 2 tablespoons
* 12 Oreos or other chocolate sandwich biscuits
* 1 tablespoon icing sugar

1. Spray baking pan with oil or nonstick spray and place in basket. 2. Preheat the air fryer to 200°C. 3. In a medium bowl, mix together the pancake mix, vanilla, and water. 4. Dip 4 cookies in batter and place in baking pan. 5. Cook for 6 minutes, until browned. 6. Repeat steps 4 and 5 for the remaining cookies. 7. Sift icing sugar over warm cookies.

Chickpea Brownies

Prep time: 10 minutes | Cook time: 20 minutes | Serves 6

* Vegetable oil
* 425 g tin chickpeas, drained and rinsed
* 4 large eggs
* 80 ml coconut oil, melted
* 80 ml honey
* 3 tablespoons unsweetened cocoa
* powder
* 1 tablespoon espresso powder (optional)
* 1 teaspoon baking powder
* 1 teaspoon baking soda
* 80 g chocolate crisps

1. Preheat the air fryer to 160°C. 2. Generously grease a baking pan with vegetable oil. 3. In a blender or food processor, combine the chickpeas, eggs, coconut oil, honey, cocoa powder, espresso powder (if using), baking powder, and baking soda. Blend or process until smooth. Transfer to the prepared pan and stir in the chocolate crisps by hand. 4. Set the pan in the air fryer basket and bake for 20 minutes, or until a toothpick inserted into the center comes out clean. 5. Let cool in the pan on a wire rack for 30 minutes before cutting into squares. 6. Serve immediately.

Simple Pineapple Sticks

Prep time: 5 minutes | Cook time: 10 minutes | Serves 4

* ½ fresh pineapple, cut into sticks
* 25 g desiccated coconut

1. Preheat the air fryer to 200°C. 2. Coat the pineapple sticks in the desiccated coconut and put each one in the air fryer basket. 3. Air fry for 10 minutes. 4. Serve immediately.

Dark Brownies

Prep time: 10 minutes | Cook time: 11 to 13 minutes | Serves 4

* 1 egg
* 85 g granulated sugar
* ¼ teaspoon salt
* ½ teaspoon vanilla
* 55 g unsalted butter, melted
* 15 g Plain flour, plus 2 tablespoons
* 30 g cocoa
* Cooking spray
* Optional:
* Vanilla ice cream
* Caramel sauce
* Whipped cream

1. Beat together egg, sugar, salt, and vanilla until light. 2. Add melted butter and mix well. 3. Stir in flour and cocoa. 4. Spray a baking pan with raised sides lightly with cooking spray. 5. Spread batter in pan and bake at 160°C for 11 to 13 minutes. Cool and cut into 4 large squares or 16 small brownie bites.

Appendix 1
Basic Kitchen Conversions & Equivalents

DRY MEASUREMENTS CONVERSION CHART

3 teaspoons = 1 tablespoon = 1/16 cup

6 teaspoons = 2 tablespoons = 1/8 cup

12 teaspoons = 4 tablespoons = 1/4 cup

24 teaspoons = 8 tablespoons = 1/2 cup

36 teaspoons = 12 tablespoons = 3/4 cup

48 teaspoons = 16 tablespoons = 1 cup

METRIC TO US COOKING CONVERSIONS
OVEN TEMPERATURES

120 °C = 250 °F

160 °C = 320 °F

180 °C = 350 °F

205 °C = 400 °F

220 °C = 425 °F

LIQUID MEASUREMENTS CONVERSION CHART

8 fluid ounces = 1 cup = 1/2 pint = 1/4 quart

16 fluid ounces = 2 cups = 1 pint = 1/2 quart

32 fluid ounces = 4 cups = 2 pints = 1 quart = 1/4 gallon

128 fluid ounces = 16 cups = 8 pints = 4 quarts = 1 gallon

BAKING IN GRAMS

1 cup flour = 140 grams

1 cup sugar = 150 grams

1 cup powdered sugar = 160 grams

1 cup heavy cream = 235 grams

VOLUME

1 milliliter = 1/5 tsp

5 ml = 1 tsp

15 ml = 1 tbsp

240 ml = 1 cup or 8 fluid ounces

1 liter = 34 fluid ounces

WEIGHT

1 gram = 0.035 ounces

100 grams = 3.5 ounces

500 grams = 1.1 pounds

1 kilogram = 35 ounces

Appendix 2

Index

A

Air Fried Chicken Potatoes with Sun-Dried Tomato········ 34
Air Fried Crab Bun ···················· 42
Air Fried Crispy Venison ···················· 23
Air Fryer Fish Fry ···················· 45
Apple Cider Doughnut Holes ···················· 4
Apple Cider Mussels ···················· 43
Apricot-Glazed Chicken Drumsticks···················· 37
Apricot-Glazed Turkey Tenderloin ···················· 34
Asian Swordfish···················· 42
Asparagus and Pepper Strata ···················· 7
Asparagus Fries ···················· 53
Authentic Scotch Eggs ···················· 17

B

Bacon and Cheese Stuffed Pork Chops ···················· 24
Bacon Wrapped Pork with Apple Gravy···················· 27
Baked Chorizo Scotch Eggs···················· 15
Baked Courgette ···················· 55
Baked Monkfish···················· 42
Baked Peach Porridge···················· 4
Baked Spanakopita Dip ···················· 19
Banger and Egg Breakfast Burrito···················· 8
Banger Egg Cup···················· 5
BBQ Prawns with Creole Butter Sauce···················· 40
Bean and Beef Meatball Taco Pizza···················· 29
Beef and Mango Skewers···················· 20
Beery and Crunchy Onion Rings ···················· 14
Berry Cheesecake···················· 11
Blackened Cajun Chicken Tenders ···················· 32
Blackened Chicken ···················· 33
Blackened Red Snapper···················· 45
Bread Rolls ···················· 52
Breaded Prawns Tacos ···················· 46
Breakfast Banger and Cauliflower···················· 6
Breakfast Meatballs ···················· 9
Broccoli Crust Pizza···················· 56
Broccoli with Sesame Dressing ···················· 50
Broccoli-Cheddar Twice-Baked Potatoes ···················· 52

Buffalo Chicken Breakfast Muffins ···················· 5
Butternut Marrow Croquettes ···················· 50

C

Cantonese BBQ Pork···················· 29
Catfish Bites ···················· 43
Cauliflower with Lime Juice ···················· 51
Celery Chicken···················· 37
Cheese Crusted Chops ···················· 24
Cheese Drops···················· 17
Cheese-Encrusted Chicken Tenderloins with Peanuts ······· 36
Cheesy Jalapeño Cornbread ···················· 15
Cheesy Roasted Sweet Potatoes ···················· 12
Cheesy Scrambled Eggs ···················· 4
Chicken and Gammon Meatballs with Dijon Sauce ········ 31
Chicken Chimichangas···················· 35
Chicken Jalfrezi ···················· 32
Chicken Legs with Leeks ···················· 38
Chicken Paillard ···················· 33
Chicken Shawarma ···················· 36
Chicken Wellington···················· 31
Chicken with Bacon and Tomato ···················· 38
Chickpea Brownies ···················· 60
Chiles Rellenos with Red Chile Sauce···················· 51
Chilli Tilapia···················· 46
Chorizo and Beef Burger ···················· 26
Cinnamon Rolls with Cream Glaze ···················· 59
Citrus Sweet Potatoes and Carrots ···················· 48
Classic British Breakfast···················· 8
Coconut Chicken Tenders ···················· 12
Coconut Prawns with Spicy Dipping Sauce···················· 40
Coriander Lime Baked Salmon ···················· 46
Cornish Hens with Honey-Lime Glaze ···················· 32
Courgette Balls ···················· 52
Crab Cake Sandwich ···················· 41
Crisp Paprika Chicken Drumsticks···················· 35
Crispy Cabbage Steaks···················· 56
Crispy Duck with Cherry Sauce ···················· 32
Crispy Filo Artichoke Triangles ···················· 18
Crispy Fried Okra with Chilli ···················· 56

Crispy Garlic Sliced Aubergine ⋯⋯⋯⋯⋯⋯ 52
Crispy Mozzarella Cheese Sticks ⋯⋯⋯⋯⋯ 21
Crispy Potato Chips with Lemony Cream Dip ⋯⋯⋯⋯⋯ 20
Crunchy Air Fried Cod Fillets ⋯⋯⋯⋯⋯⋯ 44

D

Dark Brownies ⋯⋯⋯⋯⋯⋯⋯⋯⋯⋯ 61
Drop Biscuits ⋯⋯⋯⋯⋯⋯⋯⋯⋯⋯⋯ 6

E

Easy Devils on Horseback ⋯⋯⋯⋯⋯⋯⋯ 15
Easy Greek Briami (Ratatouille) ⋯⋯⋯⋯⋯ 49
Easy Potato Croquettes ⋯⋯⋯⋯⋯⋯⋯⋯ 48
Eggnog Bread ⋯⋯⋯⋯⋯⋯⋯⋯⋯⋯⋯ 9
Everything Bagels ⋯⋯⋯⋯⋯⋯⋯⋯⋯⋯ 7

F

Fajita-Stuffed Chicken Breast ⋯⋯⋯⋯⋯⋯ 35
Fish Gratin ⋯⋯⋯⋯⋯⋯⋯⋯⋯⋯⋯⋯ 44
Five-Spice Pork Belly ⋯⋯⋯⋯⋯⋯⋯⋯⋯ 23
Friday Night Fish-Fry ⋯⋯⋯⋯⋯⋯⋯⋯⋯ 45
Fried Oreos ⋯⋯⋯⋯⋯⋯⋯⋯⋯⋯⋯⋯ 60
Fried Root Vegetable Medley with Thyme ⋯⋯⋯⋯⋯ 56

G

Garlic Butter Prawns Scampi ⋯⋯⋯⋯⋯⋯ 44
Garlic Courgette and Red Peppers ⋯⋯⋯⋯ 49
Garlic Soy Chicken Thighs ⋯⋯⋯⋯⋯⋯⋯ 34
Glazed Carrots ⋯⋯⋯⋯⋯⋯⋯⋯⋯⋯⋯ 49
Gluten-Free Muesli Cereal ⋯⋯⋯⋯⋯⋯⋯ 9
Gold Ravioli ⋯⋯⋯⋯⋯⋯⋯⋯⋯⋯⋯⋯ 56
Golden Tenders ⋯⋯⋯⋯⋯⋯⋯⋯⋯⋯⋯ 38
Greek Lamb Rack ⋯⋯⋯⋯⋯⋯⋯⋯⋯⋯ 23
Green Pepper Cheeseburgers ⋯⋯⋯⋯⋯⋯ 25

H

Ham with Sweet Potatoes ⋯⋯⋯⋯⋯⋯⋯ 28
Hawaiian Huli Huli Chicken ⋯⋯⋯⋯⋯⋯ 34
Hearty Honey Yeast Rolls ⋯⋯⋯⋯⋯⋯⋯ 6
Herbed Beef ⋯⋯⋯⋯⋯⋯⋯⋯⋯⋯⋯⋯ 25
Herbed Green Lentil Rice Balls ⋯⋯⋯⋯⋯ 20
Herbed Turkey Breast with Simple Dijon Sauce ⋯⋯⋯⋯⋯ 35
Homemade Toaster Pastries ⋯⋯⋯⋯⋯⋯⋯ 5
Honey-Apricot Muesli with Greek Yoghurt ⋯⋯⋯⋯⋯ 7
Honey-Baked Pork Loin ⋯⋯⋯⋯⋯⋯⋯⋯ 25

Honey-Mustard Chicken Wings ⋯⋯⋯⋯⋯ 21

I

5-Ingredient Brownies ⋯⋯⋯⋯⋯⋯⋯⋯⋯ 59
Indian Aubergine Bharta ⋯⋯⋯⋯⋯⋯⋯⋯ 52
Indian Mint and Chile Kebabs ⋯⋯⋯⋯⋯⋯ 27
Indian Toast and Milk ⋯⋯⋯⋯⋯⋯⋯⋯⋯ 60
Italian Chicken with Sauce ⋯⋯⋯⋯⋯⋯⋯ 36

J

Jalapeño Popper Egg Cups ⋯⋯⋯⋯⋯⋯⋯ 5
Jalapeño Poppers ⋯⋯⋯⋯⋯⋯⋯⋯⋯⋯ 18
Jalea ⋯⋯⋯⋯⋯⋯⋯⋯⋯⋯⋯⋯⋯⋯ 43
Jerk Chicken Thighs ⋯⋯⋯⋯⋯⋯⋯⋯⋯ 36
L
Lamb and Cucumber Burgers ⋯⋯⋯⋯⋯⋯ 26
Lemon-Pepper Chicken Chicken Drumsticks ⋯⋯ 19
Lettuce-Wrapped Turkey and Mushroom Meatballs ⋯⋯ 37

M

Maize and Coriander Salad ⋯⋯⋯⋯⋯⋯⋯ 50
Marinated Steak Tips with Mushrooms ⋯⋯ 25
Marinated Swordfish Skewers ⋯⋯⋯⋯⋯⋯ 40
Mediterranean Beef Steaks ⋯⋯⋯⋯⋯⋯⋯ 29
Meringue Cookies ⋯⋯⋯⋯⋯⋯⋯⋯⋯⋯ 12
Mixed Berry Crumble ⋯⋯⋯⋯⋯⋯⋯⋯⋯ 11
Mojito Lamb Chops ⋯⋯⋯⋯⋯⋯⋯⋯⋯⋯ 24
Mozzarella Bacon Calzones ⋯⋯⋯⋯⋯⋯⋯ 5
Mozzarella Cheese Arancini ⋯⋯⋯⋯⋯⋯⋯ 21
Mushroom-and-Tomato Stuffed Hash Browns ⋯⋯ 6

O

One-Dish Chicken and Rice ⋯⋯⋯⋯⋯⋯⋯ 37
Onion Pakoras ⋯⋯⋯⋯⋯⋯⋯⋯⋯⋯⋯ 17
Oyster Po'Boy ⋯⋯⋯⋯⋯⋯⋯⋯⋯⋯⋯ 43

P

Pancake Cake ⋯⋯⋯⋯⋯⋯⋯⋯⋯⋯⋯⋯ 7
Panko Catfish Nuggets ⋯⋯⋯⋯⋯⋯⋯⋯⋯ 45
Panko Pork Chops ⋯⋯⋯⋯⋯⋯⋯⋯⋯⋯ 23
Paprika Prawns ⋯⋯⋯⋯⋯⋯⋯⋯⋯⋯⋯ 45
Parmesan Banger Egg Muffins ⋯⋯⋯⋯⋯⋯ 8
Parmesan Herb Focaccia Bread ⋯⋯⋯⋯⋯ 49
Parmesan Mackerel with Coriander ⋯⋯⋯⋯ 41
Parmesan-Thyme Butternut Marrow ⋯⋯⋯⋯ 51

Parsnip Fries with Romesco Sauce · 48
Peach Fried Pies · 60
Peanut Butter Chicken Satay · 33
Pecan Rolls · 12
Peppercorn-Crusted Beef Fillet · 25
Peppery Brown Rice Fritters · 14
Peppery Chicken Meatballs · 20
Pigs in a Blanket · 24
Pitta and Pepperoni Pizza · 8
Polenta Fries with Chilli-Lime Mayo · · · · · · · · · · · · · · · · 19
Pork Bulgogi · 27
Pork Burgers with Red Cabbage Salad · · · · · · · · · · · · · · · 11
Pork Kebab with Yoghurt Sauce · 27
Pork Milanese · 26
Prawn Creole Casserole · 41
Prawns Curry · 42
Prawns Egg Rolls · 18
Puffed Egg Tarts · 11

Q

Quiche-Stuffed Peppers · 57

R

Red Lentil and Goat Cheese Stuffed Tomatoes · · · · · · · · · · · · · 14
Roasted Brussels Sprouts with Orange and Garlic · · · · · · · · · · · 50
Roasted Mushrooms with Garlic · 20
Rosemary Beetroots with Balsamic Glaze · · · · · · · · · · · · · · 55
Rosemary-Roasted Red Potatoes · 50
Rumaki · 18

S

Salmon on Bed of Fennel and Carrot · · · · · · · · · · · · · · · · · 42
Savoury Gigantes Plaki (Baked Giant White Beans) · · · · · · · · 55
Scalloped Veggie Mix · 15
Scallops in Lemon-Butter Sauce · 44
Scallops with Asparagus and Peas · 40
Sesame Carrots and Sugar Snap Peas · · · · · · · · · · · · · · · · · 48

Simple and Easy Croutons · 15
Simple Beef Mince with Courgette · · · · · · · · · · · · · · · · · · · 24
Simple Pea Delight · 14
Simple Pineapple Sticks · 60
Smoky Pork Tenderloin · 28
Southern Chilli · 28
Southwest Corn and Pepper Roast · · · · · · · · · · · · · · · · · · · 14
Southwestern Roasted Maize · 51
Spicy Lamb Sirloin Chops · 26
Spinach Omelet · 8
Steak and Vegetable Kebabs · 11
Strawberry Scone Shortcake · 59
Super Bacon with Meat · 28
Sweet and Spicy Country-Style Ribs · · · · · · · · · · · · · · · · · · 28
Sweet Potato Black Bean Burgers · 55
Sweet Potato Donut Holes · 59
Sweet Potato Fries with Mayonnaise · · · · · · · · · · · · · · · · · 19
Taco-Spiced Chickpeas · 17

T

Tilapia Almondine · 41
Tingly Chili-Roasted Broccoli · 49
Tomato and Cheddar Rolls · 9
Tuna Cakes · 41
Turkey and Cranberry Quesadillas · · · · · · · · · · · · · · · · · · · 33

V

Veggie Tuna Melts · 12

W

Western Frittata · 4

Y

Yakitori · 31

Printed in Great Britain
by Amazon